Fixing California

Pragmatism, Abundance, Optimism

By Edward Ring

ISBN 979-8543157763

Table of Contents

Preface to the 2nd Edition

This book, originally co-published by the Center for American Greatness and the California Policy Center in June and July of 2021 as a nine part series, "Fixing California," coincided with the attempt to recall California Governor Gavin Newsom. The petition to qualify a recall election was successful, and during the summer of 2021 there were dozens of individuals who stepped up as candidates to replace the governor.

While Newsom has remained in office, the topics briefly covered in this book – energy, water, transportation, housing, law enforcement and the homeless, forestry management, and education – concern policy issues that remain urgent and unresolved. The solutions recommended here are offered in a nonpartisan spirit, and remain applicable as the regularly scheduled gubernatorial election approaches in November 2022.

Fixing California is intended to provide candidates and political activists a concise vision and recipe for how to fix a critical assortment of broken policies that have all but destroyed the California dream for millions of residents.

California's prevailing political culture is premised on a world view that is comprehensively pessimistic. An entirely different approach, based on the values of pragmatism, abundance, and optimism is not merely a contrarian perspective. It is a sustainable and vastly preferable alternative that can be realized. In that spirit and towards that goal, the author hopes this book can make a small but meaningful contribution

Chapter One

Themes That Make Anything Possible

For many across America, California has become the cautionary tale for the rest of the country. Anyone who actually lives in the Golden State, and enjoys the best weather and the most beautiful, diverse scenery on earth, knows there are two sides to the story of this captivating place. Nevertheless, the story keeps getting worse.

For every essential—homes, rent, tuition, gasoline, electricity, and water—Californians pay the among the highest prices in the continental United States. Californians endure the most hostile business climate in America, and pay the highest taxes. The public schools are failing, crime is soaring, electricity is unreliable, water is rationed, and the mismanaged forests are burning like hell. Yet all of this can be fixed.

The solutions aren't mysteries.

Deregulate housing development permits.

End the disastrous "housing-first" policies and instead give the homeless safe housing in inexpensive barracks where sobriety is a condition of entry.

Repeal Proposition 47, which downgraded property and drug crimes.

Build reservoirs, desalination, and wastewater recycling plants.

Build nuclear power plants and develop California's abundant natural gas reserves.

Recognize that the common road is the future of transportation, not the past, and widen California's freeways and highways.

Let the timber companies harvest more lumber in exchange for maintaining the fire roads and power line corridors.

Implement school choice and make public schools compete with private schools on the basis of excellence.

Done.

It isn't quite that simple, of course, and in the articles to follow in this series, each of these issues will be looked at in greater depth. But while fixing California requires both political will and smarter investment of public funds (OK, *much* smarter investment of public funds), none of this can happen without a change in attitude. How we think about problems needs to change.

This isn't just about ideology. Going into that labyrinth can become a fool's errand. The politicians who governed California during what arguably were its greatest years were Democrats. Old-timers refer to them as the Pat Brown Democrats, leaders whose approach to politics was pragmatic and focused on serving the people.

During that heyday, homes were affordable and freeways weren't crowded. Public schools were good, and the University of California campuses offered the best public higher education in the country. The California Water Project, taking barely more than a decade to construct, remains the most impressive feat of interbasin water transfers in the world.

What happened?

Some of the constraints that have led to today's neglect and failures are legitimate. In the 1960s the air quality in California's urban centers, from the Santa Clara Valley to the Los Angeles Basin, was far worse than it is today, despite the fact that four times as many people are living in those basins now. Back in the

1960s, the San Francisco Bay was choking on pollution, and was on track to be filled in to make room for more suburbs.

Nobody wants to turn back the clock on an environmental cleanup that has been heroic. But today, environmentalism has gone too far. Regulations and litigation have stopped development in its tracks. More than anything else, environmentalism run amok is the reason Californians live with scarcity and high prices.

The extent and complexity of environmental regulations have allowed special interests to put their agenda ahead of the interests of ordinary Californians. Public employee unions, which didn't even exist when Pat Brown was California's governor 60 years ago, now exercise almost complete control over California's state and local government agencies. Freezing infrastructure spending allows government funds to be redirected to pay and benefits for state bureaucrats, instead of to freeways and water projects. And tying development up in knots with more regulations always means more government hiring.

Also benefiting from extreme environmentalism are California's high-tech billionaires, who now have a lucrative mandate to create an "internet of things" to monitor the consumption of resources.

Public utilities benefit because their profits (which are regulated by law at a fixed percentage of revenues) soar when the per-unit costs for electricity and water go way up to pay for renewables and to cope with artificially imposed scarcity.

This imposed scarcity keeps housing unaffordable, locking out homebuyers but yielding high returns to real estate speculators.

While this radicalized environmentalism that would have John Muir turning in his grave provides moral cover to California's economic tyrants, a similar perversion of ideals has happened with respect to race. California is one of the most unlikely places one may still find racism in the 21st century. Through the second half of the 20th century—certainly compared to every other state in America—California was not known for racism. But suddenly racism is an existential crisis. As if California's beleaguered citizens didn't have enough to contend with, now their failing public schools are moving even further from teaching the basics, turning instead to teach every subject through the lens of critical race theory.

We've heard all this before. Much of what Californians face are challenges confronting everyone in America. But California, the biggest state, and the bluest state, is a powerful trendsetter. California is broken, hijacked by opportunists wielding overwhelming financial and political power. How does this change?

The solutions to be discussed can't succeed merely on their merits, despite a compelling case for each of them. Politicians and influencers who want to fix California have to change how people think. They have to reiterate themes that change the filters through which people form opinions. California's voters are the victims of 50 years of increasingly effective brainwashing by the media, the public school system, Democratic politicians, and more recently (and more virulently than ever), by social media. They have to be deprogrammed.

The themes that will inspire Californians and alter their perception of issues might begin with the concept of abundance instead of scarcity. Californians have been convinced that rationing of water and energy and land is necessary to save the planet. But it isn't.

As will be seen, resources and technologies already exist to create abundance. There are ways to unlock open land for development, and there are ways to increase the supply and lower the price for water and electricity, without harming the environment.

Urban civilization has an inevitable footprint on ecosystems. But the solutions being proposed—thousands of square miles of wind turbines and solar farms, tens of thousands of square miles of biofuel plantations—are far worse than the conventional alternatives.

Embracing abundance and rejecting the necessity for rationing, while making a realistic assessment of the tradeoffs between various environmental solutions, are themes that cannot be emphasized enough. But other themes offer additional vital support to a new way of thinking. The Pat Brown Democrats back in the 1960s, and even a few of them today, put practical solutions ahead of ideology. Ideological extremes are hindrances to practical solutions.

Republicans and Libertarians tend to reflexively offer principled opposition to government spending on infrastructure. When they do this, they're playing into the hands of the special interests, just described, that profit when infrastructure is neglected. It isn't government spending that's bad—that judgment depends on what the spending is for.

The theme that can attract coalition partners and create majorities, building on the themes of abundance and pragmatism, is optimism. Even the liberal media ridiculed Jerry Brown as "Governor Moonbeam" when he suggested in the late 1970s that California develop its own space program.

But if Pat Brown's son didn't get much right—he is the quintessential Malthusian—when it comes to a space program in California, he was a prophet. Elon Musk has proven that. And Musk, whom libertarians tend to deride as someone who collected subsidies while building SpaceX, has—*in one decade*—

brought down the cost of lifting a payload into earth orbit by an order of magnitude. Musk is a quintessential Californian, and SpaceX is a perfect example of government funds that were invested with a tremendous return.

Optimism is an irresistible theme. With optimism, dreaming is possible, reconciliation is possible, partnerships and coalitions are possible. With optimism, abundance is not a fantasy, it is a choice, and rationing is easily overcome.

With optimism, grand bargains are possible, and big things get done. With optimism, a sense of urgency isn't oppressive, it's inspiring. Optimism is anathema to environmentalist extremists and "anti-racist" fanatics, it is the antidote to the politics of fear and resentment. Optimism, which California's ruling class has abandoned, is nonetheless in California's cultural DNA, written across the centuries.

In the chapters to follow, focusing on energy, water, transportation, housing, law and order, the homeless, forest management, and education, these themes of promise and potential still to be achieved will be woven into the narrative—because without them, nothing is possible, and with them, anything is possible.

Chapter Two

The Electric Age

If energy were abundant, clean, and sustainable, nearly every other daunting challenge facing humanity would be much easier to solve. Insufficient water? No problem. Pump more water around via inter-basin transfers and build more desalination plants. Can't convert the transportation sector to all-electric vehicles? You can if energy is abundant. Generate all the electricity you need.

Energy solves almost every other resource-related challenge facing humanity. The more energy the better. As with water, energy abundance brings with it not only more practical options in almost every economic sector, and at a lower price, but it brings resilience as well.

On the other hand, pushing all excess out of the system via conservation mandates that amount to increasingly severe rationing leaves the system—and everything that depends on it—vulnerable to catastrophe under what might otherwise be a minor disruption.

The strategic goal of California's energy planners is for the state to become "carbon neutral" as soon as possible. They view this both as an existential necessity and an achievable utopian dream. To accomplish this, California's determination to be the first developed economy in the world to go fully electric is well established.

Governor Gavin Newsom has decreed via executive order that new passenger car and truck sales have to be all-electric by 2035.[1] In this he has the enthusiastic support of the state legislature. At the same time, the legislature is making it nearly impossible to install gas appliances[2] in new homes. Expect that effort to only intensify in the coming years.

No gasoline allowed. No natural gas allowed. With those constraints, how will California ever achieve energy abundance? Gasoline, used almost exclusively as a transportation fuel, was responsible for 22 percent of the *total* energy consumed by Californians in 2019. In that same year, natural gas, which provided fuel for 43 percent[3] of California's total electricity generation, supplied 33 percent of the *total* energy consumed by Californians. Overall, natural gas and gasoline, the forbidden duo, provide over half of the energy[4] on which Californians currently rely.

To create energy abundance without natural gas or gasoline, production of every other fuel Californians use would have to double. But what are these fuels? Are they acceptable? Not really. Additional fossil fuel sources include jet fuel at 8 percent, with other petroleum and distillate fuel oil adding another 12 percent. Despite all the work of recent decades, fossil fuel is still powering well over *80 percent* of California's economy.

The challenge doesn't end there. Also out of favor is nuclear power, despite providing another two percent to the total energy Californians consume, and hydroelectric power, which adds another four percent. The favored few—biomass, solar, geothermal and wind—altogether account for only five percent of California's total energy production. As for the rest, fully nine percent[5] of California's energy comes in the form of electricity imported from other states.[6]

Understanding California's Energy Landscape

These facts represent a reality that ought to have California's legislators scratching their heads, instead of plunging headlong into additional renewables mandates and conservation schemes.

The underlying strategy is absolutely clear, but rarely expressed openly: Make energy cost so much that bleeding edge technologies can be mandated and the financing to pay for them will be covered by the consumer. And if the consumer can't afford it, special government programs will subsidize those lower income households. Middle class Californians thus get a double hit—once as ratepayers for needlessly expensive energy, and again as taxpayers who have to pay to subsidize the less fortunate.

To get an idea of how complex the process is of getting from raw energy sources—fossil fuels, nuclear, hydro, wind and solar—to actual electrons running appliances or furnaces heating homes, Lawrence Livermore Labs and the U.S. Department of Energy have produced a flow chart[7] that merits close study.

California Energy Flow - 2018
Estimated Primary Energy Consumption: 7,404 TBTU

TBTU = trillion British thermal units
7.4 TBTUs = 2.2 TWh (trillion terawatt-hours)

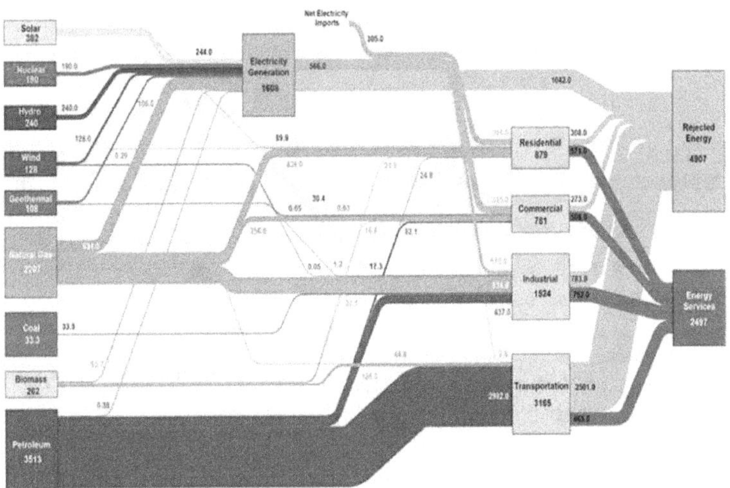

While there is a lot to digest in this energy flow chart, it offers valuable insight even without bombarding the observer with numbers. On the left, source fuel inputs are depicted, with the thickness of the lines (not the boxes) denoting the relative quantities of each fuel. Because electricity is not a source fuel, but has to be manufactured either using solar photons, or using a generator turned by wind, water, or fossil fuel, the box "Electricity Generation" shows up in the center left of the flow chart, in order to aggregate and redirect the quantities of source fuels that were converted into electricity. Further to the right, four boxes are used to aggregate and categorize what sectors make use of the various fuels including electricity, they are "Residential," "Commercial," "Industrial," and "Transportation."

It is immediately obvious that solar (yellow line) and wind energy (purple line) currently contribute an insignificant share of the total. Moreover, the method used by the study's authors to estimate the amount of solar energy contributed to the grid greatly overstates the actual amount. Their error was to take the amount of actual solar electricity generated in 2018, 27.5 gigawatt-hours which converts to 93 TBTU (trillion British thermal units), and improperly inflate it.

Instead of recognizing that photovoltaic power generation is directly transmitted to the grid without loss, the amount of solar power shown in the yellow box on the upper right of the flow chart declares 382 TBTUs of energy flowed into the grid. The reason for this error, based on a flawed assumption that is explained in the footnotes on the flow chart (which I confirmed with an electricity grid expert at the California Department of Energy), was to assume that solar power is subject to the same conversion inefficiencies as burning fossil fuel.

The implications of this are interesting. Out of 7,404 TBTUs (adjusted for the error, 7,115 TBTUs) of raw source fuels consumed, only 93 TBTUs came from solar electricity; that's 1.3 percent. That means Californians are a *long* way off from entering the solar electric age.

And yet the fact that solar electricity loses very little power when going from photovoltaic power to the grid to an EV battery to an engine is an encouraging fact. Electric transmission losses are about 10 percent, with perhaps another 10 percent lost in the onboard battery's charge/discharge cycle and the electric motor's conversion of electrons into traction. Compare photovoltaic electricity's 80 percent efficiency getting from source to end-user to the average natural gas power plant, which can only achieve efficiencies of around 42 percent,[8] or a gasoline powered automobile, which at best can achieve efficiencies of 35 percent.[9]

The consequences of energy inefficiency—the amount of source fuel inputs that are lost to excess heat and friction—are seen on the far right of the flow chart, in the box "rejected energy," which is twice as much as the box "energy services."

Of the estimated 7,404 TBTU of source fuel consumed by Californians in 2018, 4,907 TBTUs were wasted, and only half that much was enjoyed by Californians in the form of lighting, heating and air-conditioning, vehicular traction, and so on. By how much could Californians reduce the amount of fuel input, while keeping level or increasing their actual energy services, if they went totally electric?

Understanding Units of Energy Measurement

Anyone who has spent enough time reading the publications and reports that tout a clean energy future sees the marketing images: windmills presiding benignly over green pastures, solar panels glinting in the sunlight, row after row, set against a scenic horizon. But how many of California's politicians, much less the marketing consultants and graphic artists who are selling this dream, have actually tried to parse gigawatt-years into quadrillion British thermal units? It's not tough math. But it's awfully tedious.

Policymakers, along with anyone with strong opinions on California's energy policies, are encouraged to wade through these calculations, because they are crucial variables affecting the future of every Californian.

The first variable to understand is quadrillion BTUs.[10] A BTU, or British thermal unit,[11] is a measurement of energy typically used by economists. It is the amount of energy required to heat one pound of water by one degree Fahrenheit. Economists refer to the total energy consumption of entire states and nations in "Quad BTUs," which refers to 1 quadrillion (1,000,000,000,000,000) BTUs. California, in 2019, consumed 7.8 Quad BTUs of energy[12] (up five percent from 2018). Another common term is TBTU, which stands for "trillion British thermal units" (1,000 TBTUs equals 1 Quad BTU).

The second variable to understand is gigawatt-years,[13] which is a measurement unit used to measure large amounts of electricity. A gigawatt-year is the amount of electric energy that would be produced by a one gigawatt power plant, operating continuously for one year. Economists, energy planners, and utility executives typically prefer to report terawatt-hours,[14] probably since most consumers understand kilowatt-hours. But gigawatt-years is a more useful measurement of electric power.

Conceptually, these units of energy measurement are all convertible.[15] Which is to say that one Quad BTU is equivalent to 33.4 gigawatt-years, and one gigawatt-year is equivalent to 8.8 terawatt-hours.

For all units of energy, from horsepower to joules, to kilowatt-hours to British thermal units, or cubic feet of natural gas to barrels of oil, there are conversion constants that allow any unit of one form of energy to be expressed using units of another form of energy. Understanding how BTUs of natural gas or gasoline convert into electricity is necessary in order to estimate how much electricity is required to eliminate natural gas or gasoline.

The other essential concept is conversion efficiency. If every form of energy converted into another form of energy with 100 percent efficiency, the conversion constants would be all that was ever needed. But as previously noted, natural gas converts into electricity in a modern power plant at about 42 percent efficiency. Gasoline converts into traction in modern automobiles at around a 35 percent efficiency. And solar electricity can be delivered through the grid to an EV and converted into traction at around an 80 percent efficiency.

It is a fair bet that most of California's state legislators and their staffs haven't got the slightest idea how all of this works, which is why lobbyists for special interests and their useful cadres of fanatical activists (equally ignorant of energy dynamics) are so powerful.

Is a Solar Electric Economy Possible?

If you fly from California's capital city, Sacramento, southeast into Los Angeles, you'll see a growing number of sparkling greyish silver patches occupying sections of what previously was irrigated farmland in the San Joaquin Valley. These are photovoltaic arrays, ordered in row after row like crops, tracking the sun, each of them making their contribution to California's electricity grid. And catching up fast are battery farms, many of them located on the sites of decommissioned natural gas power plants, designed to soak up and store the surplus electricity generated during the hours of peak sunlight, for discharge typically in the early evening when grid demand goes up as the sun goes down.

It would go well beyond the scope of this analysis to try to precisely estimate how many TBTUs of energy input would be required to create energy abundance in a purely electric economy. But it is a relevant question to ask, since that's where current policies are taking Californians.

For a rough estimate, therefore, take the amount of actual "energy services" consumed by all four sectors of California's economy—residential, commercial, industrial, and transportation—during 2017. Assume that in an all-electric economy, instead of the reported 2,497 TBTUs of useful output requiring three times that amount of fuel input, based on the relative inefficiency of fossil fuel conversion to the various energy services, assume that only 25 percent more is required. Convert that to an electrical unit of measurement and you've got 104 gigawatt-years. Round that up to 125 gigawatt-years to be absolutely certain to achieve energy abundance.

The next thing to take into account, something heard incessantly from solar skeptics, and with good reason, is the expected amount of sunlight. Solar electricity *capacity* in California in 2019[16] was 14 gigawatts (almost all via photovoltaics, but including 1.2 gigawatts of solar thermal generating plants). But the solar electric *output* in that year was only 3.4 gigawatt-years. This disparity is due to the unfortunate reality of clouds and nighttime. By using gigawatt-years as the unit to measure total output, it is easy to see that the collective *yield* of California's solar arrays is only 24 percent. It's even less than that during the shorter daylight of winter.

According to sources at the California Energy Commission, the average performance for the large photovoltaic farms (10 megawatts and up) is an impressive 38 percent in June and July, but a dismal 13 percent in December and barely improved 16 percent in January.

What this means is that for solar power to do the whole job, the size of the solar arrays have to be scaled to generate 125 gigawatts *of continuous power* in January. We may assume that battery substations on every street corner, power walls behind every garage, and 15 million electric vehicles[17] with onboard batteries will guarantee continuous power on the smart grid. That's part of the plan. But if the sun is only delivering 13 percent efficiency, that means you need an array of photovoltaic panels big enough to collect and store enough excess power while the winter sun *does* shine to discharge at a rate of 125 gigawatts all day and all night. That means the capacity of the collective solar arrays in an electrified California would have to be 125/.13, or 961 gigawatts.

This is an almost unimaginably large quantity of solar panels. Modern photovoltaic panels will produce about 15 watts per square foot in full sun. Allowing for panels sufficient to generate 961 gigawatts, while allowing an equal amount of space for access roads, transmission lines, and other balance of plant necessities, it would take 4,600 square miles of California's land to replace natural gas and gasoline.

Can that be done? Is there room? Certainly. The sunny Mojave Desert[18] occupies 50,000 square miles, with about half of that within California. The sunny San Joaquin Valley[19] is 10,000 square miles. California has 25,000 square miles of grazing lands.[20] To suggest there isn't room for all these solar panels would be disingenuous.

Skeptics of photovoltaic power because of the space it takes up should not be suggesting there's plenty of space for new suburbs. Advocates for an explosion of photovoltaic farms should not be suggesting there is no room for new homes. California is a vast, nearly empty state. Surprisingly, because it was settled relatively late, California's 40 million people are more concentrated in urban areas[21] than any other state.

But is this desirable? Do we want to carpet an area roughly the size of Connecticut with solar panels?

Sure, solar panels could sit atop every roof and parking structure, but that wouldn't accommodate more than maybe 20 percent of the required total and those installations would be far more expensive. Yes, improvements to the photovoltaic substrate may eventually yield panels that can produce 20 watts per square foot in full sun, chopping the land required down to 3,449 square miles. That's still an awful lot of territory. And what about the heat island impact of thousands of square miles of heat absorbing dark solar collectors?

Sensible proponents might suggest limiting the state's solar share of electricity generated to the amount required during summer. In June and July, 1,573 square miles of photovoltaic arrays would fulfill 100 percent of electrified California's energy requirements, and during the rest of the year, wind power could make up the difference. But wind energy, notwithstanding the 200 tons of concrete required per tower; or the avian, insect, and bat slaughter; or the psychosis inducing thrum; or the hideous visual blight; is also intermittent.

The problem with intermittent power is that, to the extent you build intermittent power generation from wind or solar, you have to build backup systems. It would be nice to suppose that winter winds and summer sun perfectly balance the intermittency of wind generators with the intermittency of solar panels, but they don't. Whatever else you build, therefore, incurs a capital cost for continuous operation, but can only be turned on when the favored forms of electricity generation cannot deliver. Batteries can mitigate daily cycles, but not seasonal ones.

The redundant systems needed to produce electricity during, for example, windless nights in winter, don't cost less to build just because they only get turned on part-time. California's natural gas peaking plants in 2019 had a capacity of 39.4 gigawatts, but they only delivered 10.5 gigawatt-years of power. That is, they were shut down 73 percent of the time. They still cost the same amount to build. Disingenuous foes of natural gas claim electricity from natural gas is expensive. It is. But the reason is that the construction costs are being amortized over 73 percent less operating revenue than if those plants were run continuously.

The cost of a solar electric California, taking into account not only solar panels but also battery farms, conventional backup power plants, and a much more robust transmission grid, is *already* felt in the average retail price Californians pay for electricity.[22] At 22.7 cents per kilowatt hour, California shares the top spot with Connecticut. Other big states come in much cheaper. In Texas, consumers pay 11.4 cents per kilowatt hour. Even New York charges less, at 18 cents per kilowatt hour. And it doesn't end there.

To accomplish California's broader energy strategy, every home with a gas heater or gas water heater would have to be retrofitted and every gasoline powered automobile would have to be replaced. Electric charging stations would have to replace gas stations, everywhere.

The total cost would be in the hundreds of billions, if not trillions, and the ordinary consumer would foot the bill. The sheer space required for these photovoltaics, taking into account their poor performance in the winter months when there is less daylight, has to be reckoned with in any honest appraisal of solar.

How Can Energy Abundance Be Achieved?

The good news in all of this is that energy abundance is possible, and can actually be achieved at far less expense. If we strike a balance between rapid, renewables-driven electrification and an all-of-the-above approach that phases in renewable energy over a longer span of time, we can achieve energy abundance without paying exorbitant prices. California is in no danger of losing her leadership in renewables deployment, even if we slow things way down.

The urgency of the "climate emergency" inspires California's political leaders to demand precipitous changes, both to set an example to the world, and to perfect the technologies that we will roll out to the rest of the world. But developing nations are on a path towards achieving abundance for their citizens that will embrace an all-of-the-above strategy, not a strict renewables strategy. That reality is beyond serious debate. To face that reality squarely, California should set a stellar example of an all-of-the-above energy strategy. There are many elements to this.

Clearly the role of photovoltaic power is set to increase. Costs for solar panels and batteries continue to drop, at the same time as the efficiency of solar panels and the energy density of batteries continue to increase. California's legislature should fast track private development of the state's ample deposits of lithium, and confront the regulatory barriers to in-state manufacturing.

As it is, to go renewable, California currently outsources labor exploitation and environmental havoc. Bring it home, and do it right. Set the example. And face the increased costs, which ought to curb the enthusiasm for treating solar power and batteries as the one and only solution.

The concept of implementing a clean and enlightened all-of-the-above strategy as an example for the world means that California should build more nuclear power plants, embracing new technologies including reprocessing the waste and commissioning large-scale as well as smaller modular plants. Instead of dismantling its natural gas infrastructure, California should be rebuilding it, possibly taking into account that this extensive network can eventually be repurposed to transport hydrogen. California should continue to develop geothermal power, and rebuild its biomass generating capacity.

Instead of shutting down natural gas power plants, California should be converting them all to combined cycle where the excess heat drives a parallel steam turbine, allowing efficiencies of up to 60 percent.[23] California should then export these clean, ultra efficient technologies to nations like Indonesia, which isn't about to abandon fossil fuel.[24]

California should be developing its reserves of oil and natural gas; oil because pumping it here is better than importing it from Venezuela, natural gas because it is the cheapest, cleanest fossil fuel. Embracing nuclear power and clean fossil fuel as part of a portfolio of energy options is a practical route to affordable energy abundance.

Looking to the future, California should be sponsoring research into commercializing fusion energy, satellite solar power stations, hydrogen storage solutions, and next-generation biofuels that are grown and processed in factories, to name a few examples of what could come next.

More generally, California's policymakers must recognize that innovation is going to deliver energy solutions in the next few decades that we can't imagine today.

These unforeseeable energy innovations are coming, and they will not vindicate a one-dimensional renewables strategy. Rather, endless expanses of land covered with solar farms and wind turbines will be rendered obsolete, and revealed as a tremendously destructive waste.

From an economic standpoint, the strategy of rationing supply to raise prices, which in turn enables the financing of mandated, narrow solutions, is misanthropic and regressive. It is antithetical to solutions that are pragmatic, optimistic, and embrace abundance. In some cases, enabling infrastructure to create abundance requires socializing costs through general obligation bonds, which are in turn largely paid for by high income taxpayers. That is a progressive tax framework that delivers essential public amenities while sparing the low and middle income consumers. That solution may be necessary for transportation and water infrastructure. In the case of energy, however, it is largely unnecessary.

A measured all-of-the-above strategy for energy can be primarily accomplished by deregulating nuclear and natural gas energy solutions, allowing them to compete with the emerging solar, geothermal, and biomass solutions. Affordable, abundant, sustainable energy is a realistic, moral choice. It is an example California can set that the aspiring nations of the world will emulate instead of resist. And with abundant, affordable energy, everything else is possible.

Chapter Three

Achieving Abundant Water

As Californians face another drought,[25] the official consensus response is more rationing. Buy washers that don't work very well.[26] Install more flow restrictors. Move down from a 50 gallon per person, per day limit for indoor water consumption to 40 gallons per person per day.[27] For California's farmers, recent legislation has not only lowered what percentage of river flow can be diverted to agriculture,[28] but now also restricts groundwater pumping.[29] The impact is regressive, with consequences ranging from petty and punitive to catastrophic and existential.

Wealthy homeowners pay the fines and water their lawns, while ordinary citizens are forced to obsess over every drop. Corporate farm operations navigate the countless regulatory agencies while family farmers are driven insolvent. And the worse it gets, the more the story stays the same: We have wasted water, destroyed ecosystems, and now we must embrace an era of limits.[30] But this is a perilous path.

Maybe the consensus model of water management in California works for corporations that want to consolidate the agricultural industry.

Maybe it benefits developers who want to build apartments with no yards, where the interiors are equipped with "water sipping" (lousy) appliances.

Maybe the public utilities prefer a model where they don't have to build new infrastructure because per capita consumption is driven down.

Maybe the "smart growth" advocates for "infill" love the idea they can sell high density more easily because if everyone uses half as much water, twice as many households can occupy the same square mile of urban space.

But as demand is ratcheted down closer and closer to supply, the system loses all resiliency.

The concept of abundance isn't merely to preserve the lifestyles to which we have become accustomed. Abundance also protects against downside risk. What if the next drought doesn't last five years, but goes on for a few decades or more?[31] There is historical precedent for that in California, regardless of current worries about climate change. What if there's a terrorist attack, a cyberattack, a war, or another natural disaster and California's water infrastructure suffers significant damage?

Abundance means redundancy, diversity, resiliency. The case for water abundance in California is compelling not merely so California's residents can enjoy amenities that citizens of a developed, modern nation are entitled to expect. Water abundance also means Californians are better prepared for cataclysms.

This was well understood in the 1960s, when California's pragmatic Governor Pat Brown, and his successor Ronald Reagan, presided over the construction of the California Water Project,[32] which remains the most impressive system of water engineering ever built. But starting in the 1970s, when Jerry Brown (Pat's son) first became governor of California, water infrastructure became less of a priority.

For the last 40 years, apart from some investment in wastewater recycling, there has been no significant new project in California designed to *increase* the supply of water. Conservation, a commendable objective, bought Californians 40 years. In that time, the population has grown from 25 million to nearly 40 million,[33] while the supply of fresh water for people and agriculture has remained fixed.

Coming up with projects to restore water abundance to California is relatively easy: Build a few more surface storage assets, most notably the proposed Sites[34] and Temperance Flat[35] reservoirs. Upgrade and increase the capacity of existing surface storage, such as the San Luis[36] and Shasta[37] reservoirs. Complete the transition to total wastewater recycling to potable standards in all of California's major urban areas, and supplement that, especially in Southern California, with additional coastline desalination plants. Repair existing aqueducts and upgrade the Delta levees—and *voilà*, you're done.

Even at California prices, this entire assortment of major civil engineering projects could be accomplished for around $50 billion. With some of the work financed through revenue bonds, the entire debt burden on the average California household would be under $100 per year.

Creating Water Abundance in California
(MAF = million acre feet)

MAF/yr	$=B	Projects to Increase Supplies of Water
0.50	5.0	Build the Sites Reservoir
0.25	3.0	Build the Temperance Flat Reservoir
0.50	2.0	Raise the height of the Shasta Dam
1.00	7.5	So Cal water recycling plants to potable standards
1.00	15.0	So Cal desalination plants
0.50	7.5	Central and Northern California water recycling plants
1.00	7.5	Desalination plants on Central and North coasts
0.75	5.0	Facilities to capture runoff for aquifer recharge
5.50	52.5	*subtotal - water supply*
		Projects to Increase Resiliency of Water Distribution Infrastructure
	5.0	Retrofit every dam in California to modern standards
	7.5	Aquifer mitigation to eliminate toxins
	5.0	Retrofit of existing aqueducts
	7.0	Seismic retrofits to levees statewide
	24.5	*subtotal - water resiliency*
	77.0	*total - water supply and resiliency*

So why don't we do it?

For one thing, special interests benefit from politically contrived scarcity and conservation mandates. And while these special interests exploit environmentalism, that doesn't negate legitimate environmental concerns that can't be ignored. Groundwater depletion has caused land subsidence.[38] That's the real reason for salt water intrusion into the Delta, far more of a factor than the relatively negligible impact of sea-level rise. Land subsidence has also damaged California's aqueducts. And eventually depleted aquifers become so degraded they can no longer be recharged. Something had to be done.

Similarly, the health of aquatic ecosystems—California's rivers and the Delta—are not only aesthetic and moral imperatives, but have a practical impact on commercial fisheries. Balancing the need to protect the environment with the needs of agricultural and urban consumers cannot be dismissed. But none of these considerations should preclude the commencement of new projects to increase California's annual supply of water. Conservation is simply not enough.

And it is here where the role of California's environmentalist lobby has been destructive.

Environmentalists and Other Obstructionists

Environmentalists in California, unfortunately, object to virtually *every* major project that would increase the supply of water. Desalination is relentlessly attacked, despite being in use throughout the world. Environmentalist litigation is the reason that desalination plants cost two to five times[39] as much to construct in California as they do in other places, from Israel and Saudi Arabia to Singapore and Australia.

As for surface storage, even off-stream reservoirs, such as the proposed Sites Reservoir that don't impede the flow of any river, or those situated in-stream but upstream of existing dams, like the proposed Temperance Flat, or raising the height of the Shasta Dam, are anathema to environmentalists.

Objections to these projects are cases where environmentalists go too far. But they're not alone. Libertarians and, more generally, anti-tax crusaders, are also unhelpful when it comes to the infrastructure that California badly needs.

Even when projects are proposed that encounter fewer environmentalist objections, such as wastewater recycling, well-organized opponents who can't accept any government spending on infrastructure dutifully join the fray. Both of these camps, the greens and the anti-tax gangs, have acquired influence that can only be countered by a broad revision in public attitudes.

Using general obligation bonds to finance water infrastructure socializes the cost of these amenities to all Californians. By financing half of a water project with general obligation bonds, the burden to the general public is reduced.

For example, if half of a $50 billion water infrastructure budget were financed through general obligation bonds, the repayment burden on California's 13 million households[40] would only be $125 per year, and most of that would fall to the higher income groups for whom $125 means one less bottle of wine per year.

But the benefit would accrue to *all* Californians. Because the other $25 billion in revenue bonds would be matched by general obligation bonds, the rates farmers would pay for water stored behind new dams would be cut nearly in half, as would the rates that urban households would pay for desalinated or recycled water.

This is a model for affordable abundant water in California. This is the achievement that has precedent in the water projects of the 1960s and could be realized in the 2020s if there were a change in attitude and a new consensus. This is the grand bargain[41] that can inspire Californians to demand practical environmentalism and accept debt for worthy projects. This is a model to lower the cost of living.

By making California's coastal cities independent of imported water,[42] and by collecting millions of additional acre feet behind new dams during wet years to release during dry years, both farmers and California's aquatic ecosystems have far more available water. Suddenly the tradeoffs between the needs of the environment and the agricultural industry become manageable.

Pragmatic solutions exist. Beyond a new resilience, *abundance* is possible. And optimism is the fuel to make it happen.

Chapter Four

The Transportation Revolution

Reading California's "Transportation Plan 2050"[43] is a depressing journey into groupthink. Like everything coming out of the one-party bureaucracy, it is the bland product of endless meetings between "stakeholders" with the only common thread being a terror of contributing anything that might violate the pieties of climate alarm and the desperate need for "equity." The result is a Stalinesque exercise in mediocrity, without even requiring a Stalin.

Actually, mediocre may be too light a term to describe this document, because mediocre implies something relatively inert. But the recommendations this document offers in 154 pages of mind-numbing detail, will serve to *increase* the momentum of policies that are guaranteed to further impoverish Californians.

California's "Transportation Plan 2050" is consistent with a mentality that must be defeated. It is a dark vision of the future, where people will be priced out of owning and operating independent vehicles or flying, and public expenditures on transportation will be focused on modes of mass transit that are rapidly headed for obsolescence. It is a vision of the future where people of average income will be forced to live in multi-story apartment buildings and take mass transit everywhere they go, not by choice, but by economic policies and government spending choices that leave them no alternative.

As with water and energy, the conventional wisdom that governs current planning is exactly the opposite of what is coming. The conventional wisdom is that abundance—in this case in the form of inexpensive, uncongested transportation options—is impossible. But, as with water and energy, this is false. The primary reason this is false is that new technologies make the common road the *future* of transportation, not the past, and because there are leapfrog technologies that will render most forms of passenger rail obsolete within a few decades, while also taking additional pressure off of roads.

The other concept missing from California's current transportation consensus is mere practicality. It is not practical to rely on bicycles to get around. The situations where it's possible to ride a bike to work or to shop or to class or to deliver children to their activities, and so on, are *miniscule* compared to the practical necessities of life. Bike activists are yet another example of a vocal and influential minority that are given voice by activists who think that cars are ecologically unsustainable. That, too, is a myth. It is self-evident that bikes will not replace more than a minute fraction of California's transportation requirements. The case for cars is more complex but nonetheless unequivocal.

California has already seen the emergence of electric vehicles with performance specifications that outperform gasoline-powered vehicles in almost every respect. They have more horsepower, more torque, and lower maintenance. Their only weakness, and it's a big one, is that the typical electric car, even at a fast-charging station, recharges at a rate of about 10-15 miles per minute. A gasoline-powered car, to use the same comparison, recharges at a rate of about 50-100 miles per minute. For the time being, this is a flaw that will prevent universal adoption of electric vehicles.

It would be a mistake, however, to write off the potential for ongoing breakthroughs in charge-time. Lucid Motors, a Silicon Valley startup, has announced its debut vehicle will be able to charge at a rate of 20 miles per minute.[44] At that rate, EVs begin to approach refill times comparable to gasoline engines. Five minutes at the gas pump enables a 300-mile range; 15 minutes at a fast charger does the same. According to *Business Insider*, a

Chinese company has just announced an EV battery that can be fully recharged in *five minutes*.[45]

There are other objections to EVs. The environmental footprint of the EV is arguably as big as that of the gasoline-powered car. But that, too, is changing. Gasoline-powered cars, for example, are now almost completely recycled when scrapped. The same is increasingly possible for EVs, even including the batteries. Opponents of EVs are correct to point out their environmental footprint, but the same may be said about gasoline cars, as well as any form of mass transit. As EVs, and their batteries, become 100 percent recyclable, the argument is moot. *Everything* is going to have a footprint—another truth that is selectively recognized by California's allegedly green clerisy.

But making a case for EVs, green, clean, and recyclable, is only one reason that roads are the future of transportation. What about the likely possibility that combustibles will become either carbon-neutral or carbon emissions-free? Biofuel processed from algae grown in tank farms[46] that don't consume a lot of space—don't laugh, it could scale up fast—would be carbon neutral, and enable internal combustion engines to remain on the road forever. Fuel cells that run on emissions-free hydrogen, which already offer superior range when used on drones,[47] may eventually become commercially viable power plants for EVs.

These factors, some of which are likely to be realized in the near future, combined with the inevitable reality of cars that will drive themselves—freeing vehicle occupants to work, recreate, or sleep while in motion—are the reason roads are the future. Why on earth would anyone want to ride a bike to a rail station, wait for a train, marinate inside the railcars with passengers and pathogens, then walk or pedal a rent-a-bike to work, when one can simply convoy one's individual vehicle into a smart lane and without so much as looking at the road ahead—travel from doorstep to destination?

Next-generation vehicles,[48] in all sizes and configurations, have the potential to replace most if not all proposed mass transit solutions both for intercity and long-range travel. The maximum safe and sustainable cruising speed of a modern electric vehicle is conservatively pegged at 120 MPH. Vehicles of the future will not only be configured similarly to conventional cars and SUVs, they will also be mobile hotel rooms, entertainment lounges, offices, conference rooms, and buses of all sizes, offering countless levels of services. On properly designed and maintained roads, there is no reason these vehicular solutions cannot replace nearly all current or proposed modes of surface-based transit, certainly including California's high-speed rail scheme but probably including most light rail as well.

This is the choice facing Californians, a choice that is completely denied by the "visionaries" that came up with the "California Transportation Plan 2050."

There's much more.

Nowhere in this document are other imminent transportation breakthroughs even mentioned. They mention high-speed rail, not bothering to admit that California's tepid design[49] is several generations behind the fastest trains being built in the rest of the world. If we're going to build one, at least build one that's cutting edge! But making fun of high-speed rail is easy.

Instead of killing the project, an interesting twist, and something we ought to expect from leaders in a state as packed with innovators as California still is, would be to convert the miles of pylons already traversing Fresno and Kern counties into supports for a hyperloop prototype.[50]

The fastest bullet train on earth, operated by the Central Japan Railway Company, has been clocked at over 374 miles per hour.[51] California's bullet train is unlikely to even go half that fast. But a hyperloop can transport people, theoretically, at speeds in excess of jet airliners, over 500 MPH. Try that. If you're going to fund a boondoggle, at least push the envelope.

Meanwhile, however, tunneling may be another way to relieve California's congested urban boulevards and freeways. Elon Musk's Boring Company[52] is an example of a privately funded transit solution that can transport public and private vehicles point-to-point underground, moving them on and off surface streets with elevators. The Boring Company's website makes a provocative assertion: "The construction industry is one of the only sectors in our economy that has not improved its productivity in the last 50 years."

With achievements in aerospace productivity that have shocked the critics, there is no reason to doubt the revolutionary potential in Musk's assertion. His reasons? He proposes the following innovations to lower the cost of tunneling by a factor of between 4 and 10: 1) triple the power output of the tunnel boring machine's cutting unit, 2) continuously tunnel instead of alternating between boring and installing supporting walls, 3) automate the tunnel boring machine, eliminating most human operators, 4) go electric, and 5) engage in tunneling research and development.

The combination of practical innovations and an optimistic perspective are how Musk's SpaceX lowered the cost of lifting a payload into earth orbit[53] by an order of magnitude in just 10 years. Why not allow Musk's Boring Company and other tunneling innovators to go underneath California's cities, starting with Los Angeles, and create radical new ways for ordinary people, with or without their cars, to cross the city?

And while underground offers space to move through tunnels, above-ground offers space to move through the air. And again, *nowhere* in California's transportation planning is there mention of the imminent revolution in passenger drones. And just as with self-driving cars, virtually every aerospace, automotive, and high-tech company on earth is working on passenger drones. Perhaps ironically, most of the major players are operating in California. Uber has formed "Uber Air," or Elevate, to develop aerial transportation systems. Google has two companies, operating in stealth, Cora, and Kitty Hawk.[54] Also active in California are the companies Aurora,[55] in partnership with Boeing, and Vahana,[56] in partnership with Airbus.[57]

An interesting company based in Santa Cruz is Joby Aviation.[58] With an IPO imminent,[59] Joby Aviation appears to be a serious contender to deliver the first aerial taxi. Investors include Intel Capital, Toyota AI Ventures, JetBlue Technology Ventures, and Capricorn Investment Group.

This is fascinating stuff. Apparently most "air taxis" (or "sky cabs") being developed are powered by electricity, and in many respects are just enlarged versions of the drones now commonly used by hobbyists and photographers. Joby Aviation's initial aircraft design has a range of 150 miles on a single battery charge, carrying up to four passengers. The aircraft travels at relatively low altitudes to avoid having to pressurize the cabin. They are expected to be "100 times quieter during takeoff and landing than a helicopter and near-silent during flyovers."

No discussion of the imminent revolution in vehicle transportation is complete without considering the possibility of travel by land and by air in the same passenger module, with a separate wheeled module (the "skateboard") for land travel, which detaches and remains on the ground when the passenger module is lifted airborne by an independent flight module. As reported in *Electrek.co*,[60] Audi and Airbus are working on just such a solution.

Policymakers have a choice. They can recognize that private industry is creating new ways to travel on land, underground, and in the air. They can cooperate to develop uniform standards and updated laws to expedite this transformation. They can revise zoning laws, redirect funding priorities, and invest in new roads[61] and communications infrastructure. Or they can neglect road construction and instead continue to build public mass-transit systems that offer dubious prospects of ever solving growing transportation bottlenecks.

This is the enticing, bright future that is coming at California despite the pious proclamations of the political class. Where is the excitement? Where is the optimism? Instead of creating "equity" by cramming everyone into apartments and making them ride trains, why doesn't California widen the roads, add smart lanes on the freeways for high-speed autonomous vehicles, work with the FAA to designate aerial lanes for passenger drones, unleash tunneling companies to create subterranean transportation corridors, and *get out of the way*. Spending precious government funds on light rail that nobody wants to ride is a fool's errand. Declaring war on the car is shortsighted cruelty. We can do so much more.

Chapter Five

Affordable Market Housing

Everyone's heard it by now. California's got a housing shortage, with prices within 50 miles of the coast among the highest per square foot in the world. The median price of a mid-tier single-family dwelling in Santa Clara County—better known as the Silicon Valley—is now $1.4 million.[62] Statewide, the median price of a home in March was $759,000,[63] up nearly 20 percent from just one year earlier. According to Zillow, the national median price of a mid-tier single-family dwelling is $287,000,[64] barely more than one-third what the same home costs in California.

There's a perfect storm of factors causing this imbalance, which is rapidly spreading across the rest of the country. Santa Clara County's foreign-born population is an astonishing 38.5 percent.[65] In California overall, 27 percent of the population[66] is foreign-born. These millions of immigrants are bidding up the prices of housing in California.

At the same time, and with increasing voracity, major hedge funds are buying homes. It's a savvy diversification strategy. Home prices go up because people are buying them, and investment portfolios chasing yield can ride the bubble for as long as demand exceeds supply, depending on inflation to give them a soft landing if and when the market finally cools. According to a real estate consulting firm based in Southern California, one in five homes sold in 2020[67] were purchased by investors. In Orange County, 3.5 percent of all residential parcels are owned by corporations with portfolios of 200 or more properties.

But this is only half the story.

Also driving the storm is a supply chain strangled by regulations, mandates, permit delays, and excessive fees. Developers and members of builders associations in California all tell the same story: a subdivision that takes two months to get approved in Texas, and might incur a few thousand dollars in permitting fees, can take two decades to get approved in California, if it gets approved at all, and will incur millions in permitting fees.

Further catalyzing the storm are special interests, all lined up to benefit from unaffordable housing. Politically influential hedge funds have perfected the art of doing virtual inspections and can outbid individual buyers with huge down payments and pre-arranged financing. They can continue to expand their share of existing stock and exploit the benefits of buying at scale. They have no interest in seeing supply drive down prices.

The public sector as well is well served by a property bubble. When properties turn over, their values are reassessed at market rates, and property tax revenues soar. As long as building is confined to "infill," and new construction is limited, local property taxes grow commensurately. People who bought in before the run-up in values are protected by Prop. 13, which makes them relatively indifferent to the price bubble. Property owners also appreciate the opportunity to use their home equity as collateral. But the upshot of all this is people of modest income cannot afford to live in California.

How Policymakers Get Everything Wrong

To cope with unaffordable housing, California's policymakers are doing absolutely everything wrong. Their biggest mistake is to not confront the central moral argument used to justify artificial scarcity of housing, which stems from environmentalism run amok. Not one state legislator is willing to challenge the core premises of the environmentalist lobby, which are that California is running out of open space, and that new suburban developments create excessive "greenhouse gas." Both of these premises are false.

To begin with, California is a huge state, with tens of thousands of miles of undeveloped land. There are 25,000 square miles of grazing land in California, and only 8,200 square miles of urbanized land.[68] The math is almost unbelievable, but the math is simple and immutable: If you built homes for *10 million* new Californians on quarter-acre lots, and those homes were each occupied by families of four, and if you allocated an equal amount of land for roads, parks, retail establishments, and industrial parks, you would only consume 1,953 square miles. That equates to 1.2 percent of California's total land area;[69] it equates to 7.8 percent of California's grazing land; it increases California's urban footprint from 5.3 percent[70] to 6.5 percent.

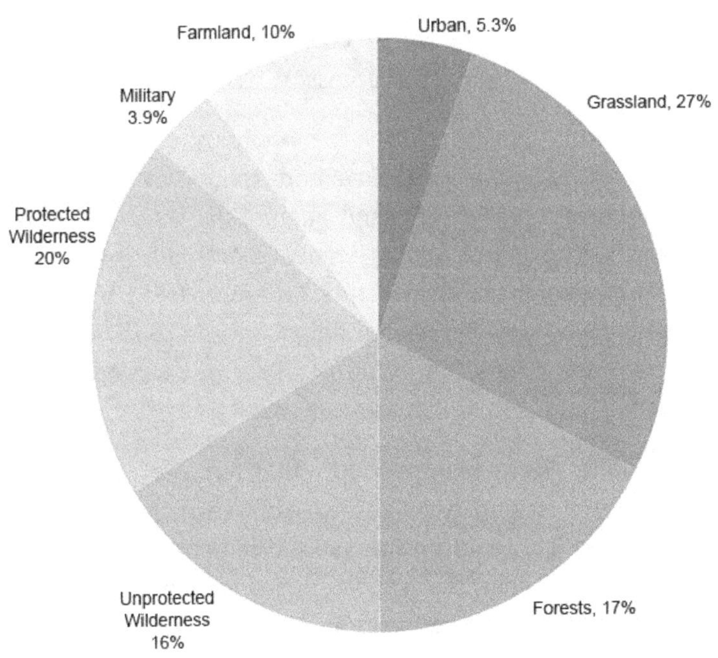

The idea that greenhouse gas emissions are increased when suburbs are built is based on biased analysis, paid for by agenda-driven activist organizations. Telecommuting, job-creating businesses migrating to new suburbs, and new, clean and sustainable modes of automotive and aerial transportation all debunk that narrative. A density delusion[71] possesses California's policymakers, and it must be broken.

In the name of stopping urban "sprawl," a cordon has been wrapped around California's cities, with increasingly aggressive state laws passed to mandate densification. Local zoning laws that residents expected to be enforced when they bought their homes are being usurped, with legislators calling yards and single-family homes "immoral." Senate Bill 9,[72] currently sailing through the California state legislature, "allows 4 market-rate homes where 1 now stands, up to 6 units if developers use a hidden 'two-step' that Livable California volunteer attorneys spotted, and 8 units with local accessory dwelling units (ADUs)."

This is California's policy solution to more housing. Use state law to empower developers and investors to buy existing single-family homes, *anywhere*, and demolish them to build apartments. This is not about "equity." It's about money. Not only will developers and investors be empowered to declare open season on any residential neighborhood, but they'll get special tax treatment and subsidies if they construct low-income housing.

That sounds very high-minded, until *you're* the family breadwinner, working two jobs to pay down your $700,000 mortgage, suddenly confronting a subsidized apartment building on the lot next to you, teeming with occupants who don't have to work and don't have to pay rent. And of course, the wealthy neighborhoods can afford to litigate, driving predatory developers to the vulnerable middle-class neighborhoods.

A Completely Different Approach to Housing

There's nothing wrong with an organic process whereby local governments recognize that certain downtown neighborhoods, or certain high-traffic boulevards, would be more appropriately re-zoned to accommodate higher density housing. That has been happening forever, and it is an inevitable fact of urban growth.

California can be the place where tantalizing possibilities[73] that urban planners dream of are realized—architectural innovations that range from "parasitic architecture"[74] to grand and inspiring new mega-structures. There is potential for high-rise, indoor agriculture;[75] there is the potential to create more *per capita* interior and exterior space, even while increasing the population per square mile. Take a look at the skyline of Dubai or Shanghai to see what a confident culture that isn't riven with Malthusian doubts and bureaucratic paralysis can accomplish.

To stabilize home prices and even begin to bring them down, however, the wood-framed one or two-story home remains a far more sustainable and cost-effective structure[76] than an urban high rise. It is also where most families *prefer* to live. And that should count for something.

The economic model that enables affordable suburbs requires a redirection of public spending and public policy. As it is, the cost of infrastructure—swollen beyond reason by excessive mandates—is paid for by the developer and passed on to the buyer in the price of the home. This can amount to hundreds of thousands of dollars once the hard costs of parks, streets, connector roads, and utility conduits are all factored into the equation. The result? Unsubsidized developers cannot make a profit building modest "mid-tier" homes that people can afford. But it doesn't have to be this way.

Public utilities could redirect just some of the money they're currently plowing into renewables to finance the energy and water infrastructure necessary for new suburbs, as well as to retrofit their existing grid. General obligation bonds and redirected monies from the state's general fund could help pay for the necessary water and transportation infrastructure. Socializing these costs, which used to be the norm, would not be prohibitively expensive if utilities, civil engineering firms, and developers had safe harbor from environmentalist litigation and excessive environmental mandates—something already done routinely for everything from sports stadiums to homeless shelters.

This is the economic model whereby the land and materials cost for new homes could be brought down significantly, at the same time as the total supply of housing would greatly increase since expansion would not only be up via infill and densification, but outwards via new suburban expansion. But curbing demand is also necessary, and can be best accomplished by using the tax system to make it less profitable for hedge funds to purchase single-family homes as investments.

The approaches necessary to bring the cost of housing down in California do not adhere to any ideological playbook. Libertarians might applaud the freedom of rural landowners to develop their properties, but object to the idea that existing zoning in residential neighborhoods should be respected. They also might not agree with a tax surcharge on properties owned by large investor conglomerates.

Ideological heresy is everywhere in this practical agenda to achieve affordable, abundant housing. Issuing bonds or allocating government funds to build water and transportation infrastructure will further inflame the anti-tax lobby. Developing open land and slowing down the deployment of renewables will infuriate the environmentalist lobby. But these are the practical, bipartisan steps that will make California's housing affordable again.

It is possible for ordinary Californians to again be able to realize the dream of home ownership in upgraded, modern, glorious, sprawling, glittering cities and suburbs. It is possible to find a new balance between environmental concerns and the aspirations of California's 40 million residents. It is possible to find a balance between urban densification and suburban expansion. It is possible to redirect government spending to build the infrastructure to make the enabling elements of urban growth—energy, water, and transportation—abundant and affordable again.

This is the optimistic, pragmatic vision that offers an alternative to the Malthusian, special interest-dominated agenda that currently governs Sacramento legislators. It must be advocated relentlessly and without reservations, because it is the path to a bright and prosperous future for everyone.

Chapter Six

Law Enforcement and the Homeless

The homeless population in California now tops 160,000,[77] concentrated in Los Angeles County, but growing in every major city and in smaller towns up and down the state. Despite throwing tens of billions[78] of federal, state, and local spending at the problem, the number of homeless increases every year. Expensive housing is part of the problem, and increasing the supply and lowering the cost of homes might help.

It is a huge mistake, however, to claim that a shortage of housing is the primary cause of homelessness in the Golden State. After all, during 2021 an estimated 103,000 new housing units[79] were built in California, slightly more than half of them homes and the rest apartments. Meanwhile, California's total population actually declined by 182,000 people,[80] the first time that's happened in over a century.

There must be more to this puzzle than housing, and there is: California's homeless problem is caused by the inability of law enforcement and health professionals to deal effectively with criminals, substance abusers, and the mentally ill. If these people were taken off the streets and treated appropriately, the remaining homeless could easily be accommodated by existing shelter programs. Solving the homeless crisis requires reassessing the underlying assumptions informing the policies of recent years, rethinking the nature and meaning of compassion, and recalibrating where tolerance ends and law enforcement begins.

As it is, the so-called "housing first" policy has been a disaster. It has spawned a Homeless Industrial Complex[81] of developers, public bureaucrats, and assorted "nonprofits" who have squandered billions on supportive housing and shelters that are outrageously expensive and place little or no requirements on occupants. The average per-unit cost for "permanent supportive housing" has been well over $500,000,[82] and at that price, only a small fraction of California's homeless have gotten under a roof.

Meanwhile, from Venice Beach to downtown San Francisco, and in countless other neighborhoods and urban cores, junkies, alcoholics, schizophrenics, and predators are sleeping, shitting, and shooting up in plain sight. It is an environmental, health, and safety catastrophe, and the situation is worse than ever.

How Did the Homeless Crisis Get So Bad?

An assortment of policy failures can be directly linked to why homelessness in California is a bigger problem than ever. They have taken the form of overzealous court rulings, citizen-approved ballot measures that wreaked havoc in their unintended consequences, and flawed legislation.

Court Decisions: The Ninth U.S. Circuit Court of Appeals, unsurprisingly, is the author of at least three rulings that have tied the hands of law enforcement in dealing with the homeless. The most significant of these is *Jones* v. *the City of Los Angeles*,[83] decided in 2006, which ruled that law enforcement and city officials can no longer enforce the ban on sleeping on sidewalks anywhere within the Los Angeles city limits until a sufficient amount of permanent supportive housing could be built. Subsequent to the *Jones* ruling, activist attorneys repeatedly have sued cities and counties to force them to define "permanent supportive housing" with specifications that make it far more difficult and expensive to get anything built.

The practical impact of these rulings is to create private space wherever a homeless person camps on publicly owned property. Apart from trying—often ineffectively—to prevent the homeless from blocking passage on roads and sidewalks, if a homeless person wants to camp in a public space, that person cannot be removed.

State Ballot Initiatives: In 2014 California voters approved Proposition 47,[84] which downgraded drug and property crimes. Proposition 47 has led to what police derisively refer to as "catch and release," because suspects are only issued citations with a court date, and let go. With respect to the homeless, passage of this initiative has made it a waste of time for police to arrest anyone for openly using illegal drugs or for petty theft (defined as stealing items worth less than $950 *per day*). Only very serious crimes are still investigated. Proposition 47 has enabled anarchy among the homeless and in the neighborhoods where homeless are concentrated.

In 2016, California voters approved Proposition 57,[85] intended to make state prison inmates convicted of nonviolent felony crimes eligible for parole. About 7,000 inmates immediately became eligible, and as of early 2016, there were about 25,000 nonviolent state felons who could seek early release and parole under Proposition 57. We can hope that most of these released inmates reintegrated successfully into society. But those among this at-risk population who did not reintegrate joined California's homeless.

State Legislation: Foremost among recent state laws that have exacerbated the homeless problem is AB 109,[86] passed in 2011, which released tens of thousands of "nonviolent" criminals out of county jails due to overcrowding without providing adequate means to monitor and assist their transition back into society. Thousands of these inmates were coping with drug addiction and mental illness, and they have found their way onto California's streets and public spaces. Many of them are "non-violent" drug dealers or convicted thieves. As with Proposition 57, AB 109 has changed the character of California's homeless population.

No summary of counterproductive state legislation would be complete without mentioning the laws that make it nearly impossible to get treatment for mentally ill homeless people.

According to a report published by *CalMatters*,[87] this problem began way back in 1967 with "a law signed by then-Governor Ronald Reagan. Aimed at safeguarding the civil rights of one of society's most vulnerable populations, the Lanterman-Petris-Short Act[88] put an end to the inappropriate and often indefinite institutionalization of people with mental illnesses and developmental disabilities."

Ever since, and especially in recent years as the percentage of homeless who suffer from mental illness has increased, attempts to reform the Lanterman-Petris-Short Act have faced tenacious resistance from the ACLU and other homeless advocacy groups.

As reported by San Francisco's public radio station KQED,[89] during 2018 three laws were introduced by California legislators that would "attempt to change conservatorship rules to allow city health workers to help homeless people with substance abuse and mental health problems by legally and temporarily stepping in to force a mentally ill person into treatment."

Only one, SB 1045,[90] became law, and the final version was so watered down that San Francisco's Mayor London Breed, a liberal Democrat, claimed,[91] "As drafted, SB 1045 would allow us to help fewer than five individuals." As of May 2021, the official estimates of the number of homeless in San Francisco ran as high as 20,000.[92]

The Obligations of Compassion

Exercising what *City Journal*'s Christopher Rufo calls "unlimited compassion"[93] for the homeless has been a disaster. What informs homeless policies, especially in California cities governed by progressives, seems to come down to this: homelessness and crime are problems we just have to live with until we've achieved equity and social justice for all.

The new breed of Democratic prosecutors who embrace this theory—including George Gascón[94] in Los Angeles County and Chesa Boudin[95] in San Francisco—are part of the problem, not the solution. They have placed a highly selective compassion before common sense.

It is true that Americans need to figure out how to reduce the number of people who are incarcerated. But the obligations of common-sense compassion require policymakers to accept unpleasant realities: When you downgrade crimes you encourage more crime. When you decriminalize possession and personal use of hard drugs, you encourage more drug addiction. When you provide benefits and services to homeless people, you encourage more homelessness.

These realities don't mean we shouldn't have compassion for people who are homeless or who are coping with drug addiction, or even for those who have turned to a life of crime. But creating incentives for people to be homeless, or drug addicts, or criminals is a recipe for a failed state.

A return to broken windows policing,[96] in the broadest sense of that term, would have a deterrent effect. The crime and drug use and homelessness that remained would be manageable, especially if the power of the Homeless Industrial Complex is broken. Instead of building half-million-dollar apartments in the most expensive parts of our cities, officials could construct supervised tent encampments in more affordable areas.

Compassion has become so corrupted by progressives and the special interests who *benefit* from disorder and misery that the policies enacted in its name have made the problem worse. How is it compassionate when supposedly compassionate policies lead to more victims: more homeless, more drug addicts, more criminals?

Compassion, properly tempered with common sense, and properly balanced with the other fundamental moral values, may seem harsh, but the results are what matter, not the rhetoric.

Paul Webster, who until 2020 operated a privately funded homeless shelter in San Diego, has described how there are two ways to treat the homeless, the "transformation model" and the "containment model." The transformation model works to identify homeless individuals who are able to transition back to self-sufficiency and gives them the training and services to accomplish that. The containment model emphasizes getting shelter for the homeless before offering additional services.

Webster's organization, Solutions for Change,[97] requires no drug use and work; they have roommate restrictions, partying restrictions, and they do drug testing. This means they can't accept federal funds and they also aren't eligible for state funds because of the "housing first" rule, meaning that housing has to be provided before providing any other solutions to homelessness. After a bitter fight with federal authorities seeking to enforce the "housing first" doctrine, the organization was forced to abandon drug testing[98] in some of its locations, against the wishes of the residents.

This is lunacy. According to Webster, there are three types of homeless. About 15 percent are "cannots" who are mentally ill or disabled. Another 40 percent or so are the "have nots"— people who could succeed if they were trained to acquire new skills and had access to services. The have-nots are often not counted; they live doubled up in homes, with friends, in cars. Many of them are single mothers who want to avoid living on the street. The remaining roughly 45 percent, and easily the majority of the "unsheltered" homeless, are the "will nots" who do not want to change. Most of these are drug addicts or alcoholics. They're the most problematic of the three.

The will-nots know they have safe havens on the street, where they can get drugs cheaply and readily. The will-nots become very sophisticated at getting things for nothing—the government doesn't make a distinction between the unwilling and the unable—as a result the unwilling will always have the ability to crowd out the unable.

Because of laws aimed at helping the homeless (the Federal Hearth Act)[99] or at criminal justice reform (California's Proposition 47 and AB 953),[100] the will-nots generally receive the bulk of government services, despite the fact that their treatment is invariably more expensive, and the likelihood they will ever change is small. Left behind are the cannots and the have-nots. Also left behind, at least when it comes to funding, are organizations that work on permanent transformation, instead of mere containment.

To state the obvious, all of this must change. Here are some ways to make that happen.

Solutions to America's Homeless Crisis

Quit blaming homelessness on prejudice and privilege.

According to the National Alliance to End Homelessness, African Americans make up 13 percent of the general population, but more than 40 percent of the homeless population. Similarly, American Indians/Alaska Natives, Native Hawaiians and Pacific Islanders, and people who identify as two or more races make up a disproportionate share of the homeless population. Clearly, minority communities are disproportionately represented among the homeless.[101]

While these statistics are probably accurate, they are used to reinforce the liberal catechism that finds all disparities between minorities and whites to be the result of white racism. Accepting this catechism results in policies that are ineffective, expensive, and divisive. Rather than granting preferences and entitlements to people based on their alleged status as victims of racism, it would be far more productive to identify the more likely cause of individual criminality, addiction, and unemployability, which is the parental status of the homes they grew up in.

For example, 57 percent of black children in 2014 were being raised by single mothers, compared to only 18 percent of white children. There is a remarkable degree of correlation between the proportions of homeless by race, and the proportions of single parent households by race.

It's easy, and plays well, to attribute minority homelessness to racism. But a growing body of evidence suggests that intact families are the prevailing indicator of individual success in life. Until that evidence is confronted by the communities affected by it, other suggested causes for minorities being disproportionately represented among the homeless lack authenticity.

Untie the hands of law enforcement.

The theory of "broken windows," or "order maintenance" policing argues that "tolerating too much local disorder created a climate in which criminal behavior, including serious crimes, would become more likely, since criminals would sense that public norms and vigilance were weak."[102] Broken Windows policing, whereby police crackdown on low-level crimes, was begun in the 1990s in New York City and—so long as it remained in effect—was credited with greatly reducing crime rates.

At the other extreme is the near lawlessness that prevails today on the streets of Seattle, San Francisco, Los Angeles, and other cities experiencing a homeless crisis. In California, as described, well-intentioned citizen-approved ballot measures and ill-conceived legislation have tied the hands of law enforcement. Public intoxication, petty crime, and vagrancy are all either decriminalized or have been downgraded to the point where offenders have to be released almost immediately after apprehension.

The consequences of tying the hands of law enforcement are obvious. It is preposterous that criminals, drunks, drug addicts, and insane people are permitted to take over entire sections of cities and neighborhoods, but that's exactly what's happened. It is important to stress that while a little over 40 percent of the homeless are so-called "have nots," these people almost all find shelter, often with friends or family. The remainder, the "cannots" and the "will nots," are the ones found living on the streets. Virtually all of these "cannots" and "will nots" are either mentally ill, alcoholics, or drug addicts; many of them are criminals.

Measures that tie the hands of police have to be overturned by voters or repealed by the legislature. Police need to be allowed to do their jobs.

Make it easier to commit the mentally ill.

It's worth wondering how anyone can think it is compassionate to allow raving schizophrenics, terrified by their own thoughts, to roam unmedicated on crowded city streets. But that's what's been happening in the interests of protecting their human rights. Certainly, it is important to avoid overreach, but at this point laws available to compel the mentally ill into treatment are inadequate. Often the afflicted have family members who have the means to help and are desperate to get their relatives into treatment, but the laws prevent them.

Approximately 15 percent of the homeless are mentally ill; arguably, the alcoholics and drug addicts are also suffering from a form of mental illness. Together these cohorts constitute well over half of all homeless, and nearly all of the unsheltered homeless seen on the streets. Families, caseworkers, and mental health professionals need to be given the legal tools to help these people.

Overturn Jones v. the City of Los Angeles and similar court rulings.

Starting in 2006 with the Ninth Circuit's decision in *Jones*,[103] the homeless cannot be prohibited from sleeping on the street unless "permanent supportive housing" is available. The impact of these rulings, combined with the other constraints on law enforcement, make it nearly impossible to clear the streets of homeless encampments.

The problem has been exacerbated by subsequent lawsuits to enforce the *Jones* decision, the cumulative effect of which has defined "permanent supportive housing" in ways that make it more expensive. The practical impact of the *Jones* case has been to make it financially impossible to ever deliver adequate housing alternatives to the homeless. A major city with the financial wherewithal to pay for a sustained legal battle needs to challenge the *Jones* decision all the way to the U.S. Supreme Court, with the objective being a ruling that will permit less elaborate, more cost-effective housing and shelter solutions to be allowable alternatives.

Set limits on costs.

In Los Angeles today, temporary shelter (designed to last three years) is being constructed at a cost of just over $50,000 per bed, and "permanent supportive housing" units are being constructed for more than $400,000 each on average. These costs are absurd. Designing solutions that cost less, but offer shelter to 100 percent of the homeless, is vastly preferable to solutions that cost so much that only a fraction of the homeless get assistance.

Low-cost creative solutions exist. Off-the-shelf tents, sheds, prefab "tiny homes," and prefab homes made from shipping containers are all less costly options. Relocating the homeless to repurposed industrial or retail sites that are already built out and not on premium real estate would cut costs.

Putting shelters in the middle of some of the most expensive real estate on earth not only squanders finite available funds, but when the unused property is government-owned, the chance is lost to sell that property and invest the proceeds in less expensive locations. Somehow, the public needs to pressure politicians to recognize that costs are out of control and act accordingly.

Assert the moral argument for a new approach.

Most citizens who live in neighborhoods or commercial centers overrun with homeless people feel justifiable anger at the failure of civic leaders to get the problem under control. But no serious conversation about solutions should fail to acknowledge the fact that the homeless are people who deserve compassion. For every predator, opportunist, or slacker, there are others who have simply lost their way. Who knows what happened during the formative years of an inmate just thrown back onto the streets, or a teenager who just aged out of foster care?

When discussing new policies to manage the problem of homelessness, the importance of compassion can remain first among equals when considered along with other moral virtues;[104] fairness, loyalty, authority, sanctity, and liberty. When offering new solutions, practical solutions, solutions that work for *everyone* affected by homelessness, reformers have to emphasize the moral worth of their ideas. They may have to shout this over the well-orchestrated objections coming from the compassion brigades. But fighting the compassion brigades does not require one to lack compassion.

The culture of normalizing drug use, protecting the rights of the mentally ill to their detriment, insisting on prohibitively expensive accommodations for the homeless—these are all morally flawed arguments. The deterrent value of strictly enforced laws against vagrancy has moral worth, because individuals—specifically, the "will nots"—will not be enabled to more easily choose a life of idle indulgence. Compelling the mentally ill to submit to treatment is a humane policy, not oppression. Similarly, compelling addicts and alcoholics into treatment facilities where they can detox and work productively is often the only way to offer them a chance to recover their dignity and regain control of their lives.

Part of this moral conversation must examine the wisdom of the "housing first" policy of containment that is now a condition of receiving federal funds for homeless programs. Proponents of new approaches to helping the homeless should consider the success of transformational programs, which offer job training, counseling, and sobriety programs in addition to shelter.

When discussing the moral worth of a new approach to combating homelessness, perhaps the most urgent priority is to end the waste and corruption that infest the entire process today. The absurd costs of any sort of construction is exacerbated by the myriad parties to the process, all with their hands out, all of them hiding behind righteous rhetoric. The Homeless Industrial Complex has spawned far too many charlatans and opportunists. They must be exposed and expelled.

In California, a Homeless Industrial Complex has acquired money and power by presiding over a problem that has only gotten worse, year after year. The worse the problem has gotten, the more money and power they have acquired. Creative solutions exist, and only await a critical mass of networked citizens and conscientious policymakers to insist on change.

Chapter Seven

Forest Management

Nobody knew how the fire started. It took hold in the dry chaparral and grasslands and quickly spread up the sides of the canyon. Propelled by winds gusting over 40 miles per hour and extremely dry air (humidity below 25 percent), the fire spread over the ridge and into the town below. Overwhelmed firefighters could not contain the blaze as it swept through the streets, immolating homes by the hundreds. Even brick homes with slate roofs were not spared. Before it finally was brought under control, 640 structures including 584 homes had been reduced to ashes. Over 4,000 people were left homeless.

Does this sound like the "new normal?" Maybe so, but this description is of the Berkeley fire of 1923.[105] In its time, with barely 4 million people living in California, the Berkeley fire was a catastrophe on par with the fires we see today.

When evaluating what has happened nearly a century since the Berkeley fire, two stories emerge. The story coming from California's politicians emphasizes climate change. The other story, which comes from professional foresters, stresses how different forest management practices might have made many of the recent fires far less severe—and perhaps avoided entirely.

Specifically, California's misguided forest management practices included several decades of successful fire suppression, combined with a failure to remove all the undergrowth that results when natural fires aren't allowed to burn.

Back in 1923, tactics to suppress forest fires were in their infancy. But techniques and technologies improved apace with firefighting budgets. By the second half of the 20th century, an army of firefighters could cope very effectively with California's wildfires. The result is excessive undergrowth, which not only creates fuel for catastrophic and unmanageable superfires, but competes with mature trees for the sunlight, water, and soil nutrients needed for healthy growth.

This is the real reason why California's forests are not only tinderboxes but are also filled with dying trees. Now Californians confront nearly 20 million acres of overgrown forests.

By the time you read this, Californians may be coping with yet another round of superfires. During the 2020 fire season,[106] an estimated 4.2 million acres burned, the most since recordkeeping began. To put this into perspective, this is more than 6,500 square miles, an area nearly the size of the State of New Jersey.[107]

To gauge the extent of the devastation, relying on the square miles of the containment areas may be somewhat misleading. Drive up Highway 70 in the Feather River Canyon today and note that while all of it was designated as burned, the destruction was uneven, with some hillsides left intact while others were scorched.

But there is no question that some of the most devastating fires in modern history have hit California in recent years, killing hundreds, displacing thousands, and costing billions.

Clearly, when the state faces multi-year droughts, the summer fire risk gets progressively worse. In such conditions, a few lightning strikes can spark a conflagration. But during the 2020 fire season, why is it that the Creek Fire consumed nearly 400,000 acres[108] and displaced over 12,000 people, but spared the forests surrounding Shaver Lake? What happened?

It wasn't luck. The forests around Shaver Lake had been carefully managed for decades.[109] The undergrowth was regularly thinned, either mechanically or through controlled burns, and mature trees were selectively logged. These practices nurtured an ecosystem that was, and remains, healthier and more diverse than those found even in forests that remain untouched by fires. Why aren't all of California's forests managed the way Shaver Lake is managed?

Negligence, not Climate Change, Causes Superfires

In 2019, President Trump tweeted, "The Governor of California, @GavinNewsom, has done a terrible job of forest management." Newsom tweeted back, "You don't believe in climate change. You are excused from this conversation."[110]

Meanwhile, former California Governor Jerry Brown addressed Congress in October 2019, saying, "California's burning while the deniers make a joke out of the standards that protect us all. The blood is on your soul here and I hope you wake up, because this is not politics, this is life, this is morality. You've got to get with it—or get out of the way."[111]

Despite California's current and former governors both being ardent members of the catastrophe chorus, climate change is *not* the primary cause of California's recent superfires. Newsom, Brown, other extreme environmentalists, and the policies they demanded, are the reason California's wildlands are going up in flames. They are the ones who need to be excused from the conversation. They are the ones who need to get out of the way. They are the ones who are in denial.

For about 20 million years, California's forests endured countless droughts, some lasting over a century. Natural fires, started by lightning and very frequent in the Sierras, were essential to keep forest ecosystems healthy. In Yosemite, for example, meadows used to cover most of the valley floor, because while forests constantly encroached, fires would periodically wipe them out, allowing the meadows to return. Across millennia, fire-driven successions of this sort played out in cycles throughout California's ecosystems.

Also for the last 20 million years or so, climate change has been the norm. To put this century's warming into some sort of context, Giant Sequoias once grew on the shores of Mono Lake. For at least the past few centuries, forest ecosystems have been marching into higher latitudes because of gradual warming. In the Sierra Foothills, oaks have invaded pine habitat, and pine, in-turn, have invaded the higher elevation stands of fir. Today, it is mismanagement, not climate change, that is the primary threat to California's forests.

This can be corrected.

In a speech before Congress[112] in September, Representative Tom McClintock (R-Calif.) summarized the series of policy mistakes that are destroying California's forests.[113] McClintock's sprawling 4th congressional district[114] covers 12,800 square miles, and encompasses most of the Northern Sierra Nevada mountain range.[115] His constituency bears the brunt of the misguided green tyranny emanating from Washington, D.C. and Sacramento.

"Excess timber comes out of the forest in only two ways," McClintock said. "It is either carried out or it burns out. For most of the 20th Century, we carried it out. It's called 'logging.' Every year, U.S. Forest Service foresters would mark off excess timber and then we auctioned it off to lumber companies who paid us to remove it, funding both local communities and the forest service. We auctioned grazing contracts on our grasslands. The result: healthy forests, fewer fires and a thriving economy. But beginning in the 1970s, we began imposing environmental laws that have made the management of our lands all but impossible. Draconian restrictions on logging, grazing, prescribed burns and herbicide use on public lands have made modern land management endlessly time-consuming and ultimately cost-prohibitive. A single tree thinning plan typically takes four years and more than 800 pages of analysis. The costs of this process exceed the value of timber—turning land maintenance from a revenue-generating activity to a revenue-consuming one."

When it comes to carrying out timber,[116] California used to do a pretty good job. In the 1950s the average timber harvest in California was around 6.0 billion board feet per year. The precipitous drop in harvest volume came in the 1990s. The industry started that decade taking out not quite 5 billion board feet, and by 2000 the annual harvest had dropped to just over 2 billion board feet. Today, only about 1.5 billion board feet per year come out of California's forests as harvested timber.

Expand the Timber Industry

What McClintock describes as a working balance up until the 1990s[117] needs to be restored. In order to achieve a sustainable balance between natural growth and timber removals, California's timber industry needs to *triple* in size. If federal legislation were to guarantee a long-term right for timber companies to harvest trees on federal land, investment would follow.

Today only 29 sawmills remain in California, along with eight sawmills that are still standing but inactive. In addition, there are 112 sites in California where sawmills once operated. In most cases, these vacant sites of former mills are located in ideal areas for rebuilding mills and resuming operations.

The economics of reviving California's timber industry are compelling. A modern sawmill with a capacity of 100 million board feet per year requires an investment of $100 million. Operating at a profit, it would create 640 full-time jobs. Constructing 30 of these sawmills would create roughly 20,000 jobs in direct employment of loggers, haulers, and mill workers, along with thousands of additional jobs in the communities where they are located.

California's Sawmills - 2020

29 active (1.6 BBF/year), 8 idle
There are 112 additional sites where sawmills once operated.

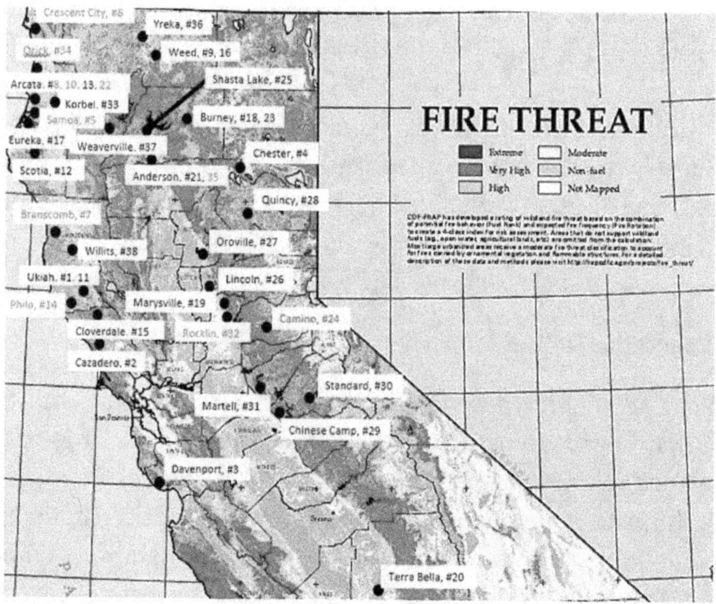

The ecological impact of logging again in California's state and federal forests will not become the catastrophe that environmentalists and regulators once used as the pretext to all but destroy that industry. Especially now, with decades of accumulated experience, logging does more good than harm to forest ecosystems. There is ample evidence to prove it.

In forests managed by Sierra Pacific, for example, owl counts are higher than in California's federally managed forests. Even clear-cutting, because it is done on a 60- to 100-year cycle, does more good than harm to the forests. By converting one or two percent of the forest back into meadow each year, areas are opened up where it is easier for owls to hunt prey. Also, during a clear cut, the needles and branches are stripped off the trees and left to rejuvenate the soil. The runoff is managed as well, via contour tilling which follows the topography of the hillsides. Rain percolates into the furrows, which is also where the replacement trees are planted.

How the Forests Surrounding Shaver Lake Were Saved

While clear-cutting will not destroy most ecosystems, since it is only performed on one to two percent of the land in any given year, there are other types of logging that can be used in areas deemed more ecologically sensitive. Southern California Edison owns 20,000 acres of forest around Shaver Lake in Southern California where they practice what is known as total ecosystem management.

Earlier this year, when the Creek Fire burned an almost unthinkable 550 square miles in Southern California, the 30 square mile island of SCE managed forest around Shaver Lake was unscathed.[118] This is because for decades, SCE has been engaged in timber operations they define as "uneven age management, single-tree selection," whereby the trees to be harvested are individually designated in advance, in what remains a profitable logging enterprise. Controlled burns are also an essential part of SCE's total ecosystem management, but these burns are only safe when the areas to be burned are well-managed with logging and thinning.

The practice of uneven age management could be used in riparian canyons, or in areas where valuable stands of old-growth trees merit preservation. The alternative, a policy of hands-off preservation, has been disastrous. Tree density in the Sierra Nevada is currently around 300 per acre, whereas historically, a healthy forest would only have had around 60 trees per acre. Clearly, this number varies depending on forest type, altitude, and other factors, but overall, California's forests, especially on federal lands, contain about five times the normal tree density. The result is trees that cannot compete[119] for adequate moisture and nutrients, far less rain percolating[120] into springs and aquifers, disease and infestation of the weakened trees, and fire.

This alternative—manage the forest or suffer fires that destroy the forest entirely—cannot be emphasized enough. In the Feather River Canyon, along with many other canyons along the Sierra Nevada, the east-west topography turned them into wind tunnels that drove fires rapidly up and down the watershed. Yet these riparian areas have been among the most fiercely defended against any logging, which made those fires all the worse. The choice going forward should not be difficult. Logging and forest thinning cannot possibly harm a watershed as much as parched forests burning down to the soil, wiping out everything.

Expand the Biomass Power Industry

If removing trees with timber operations is essential to return California's forests to a sustainable, lower density of trees per acre, mechanical removal of shrub and undergrowth is an essential corollary, especially in areas that are not clear cut. Fortunately, California has already developed the infrastructure to do this. In fact, California's biomass industry used to be bigger than it is today, and can be quickly expanded.

Today there are 22 active biomass power plants in California, generating just over a half-gigawatt of continuous electric power. That's one percent of California's electricity draw at peak demand; not a lot, but enough to matter. Mostly built in the 1980s and '90s, at peak, there were 60 biomass power plants in California, but with the advent of cheaper natural gas and cheaper solar power, most of them were shut down. These clean-burning plants should be reopened to use forest trimmings, as well as agricultural waste and urban waste as fuel.

California's Biomass Power Plants - 2020

22 active (562 MW), 14 idle (260 MW, blue)
Circles indicate 30 mile economic viability zone

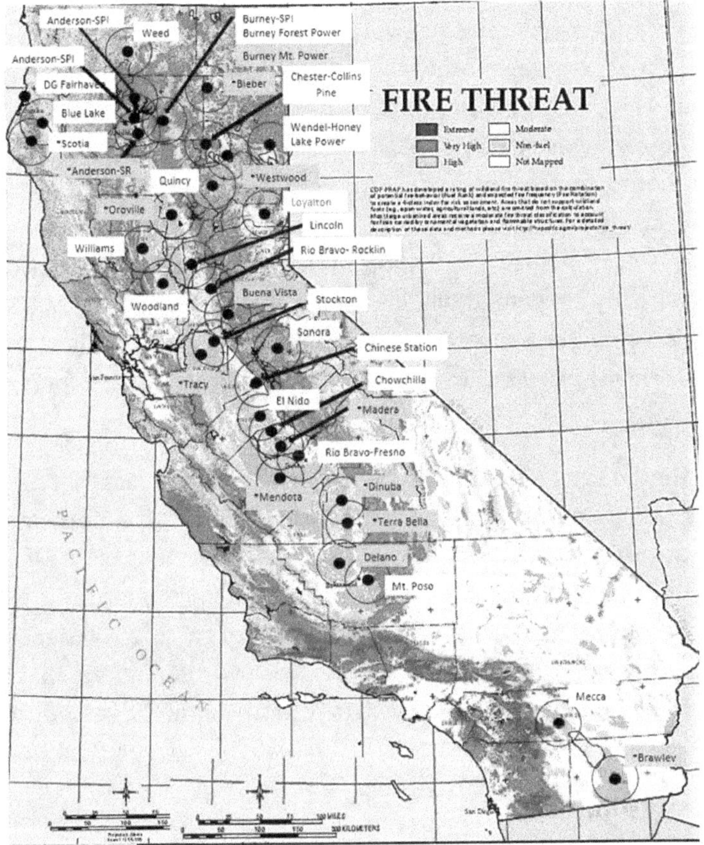

At a fully amortized wholesale cost estimated somewhere between 12 cents and 14 cents per kilowatt-hour, biomass power plants cannot compete with most other forms of energy. But this price is not so far out of reach that it could not be subsidized using funds currently allocated to other forms of renewables, infrastructure, or climate change mitigation. Moreover, this kilowatt-hour price necessarily includes the labor-intensive task of going into the forests and extracting the biomass, creating thousands of good-paying jobs. The numbers could work.

If, for example, biomass power capacity in California were roughly doubled to one gigawatt of continuous output, a six cents per kilowatt-hour subsidy would cost about $500 million per year. This must be compared to the annual cost of wildfires in California, which easily exceeds a billion per year. It also must be compared to the amount of money being thrown around on projects far less urgent than rescuing California's forest ecosystems, such as the California High Speed Rail project, which has already consumed billions. And if this entire subsidy of $500 million per year were spread into the utility bills of all Californians, it would only amount to about a 1.5 percent increase.

Further in support of this economic analysis is the fact that much of the kilowatt-hour price for biomass electricity is amortization of the initial construction cost of the generating plant. If, as appears likely, Americans endure another multi-year bout with broad-based inflation, that fixed amortization cost will become less significant as all electricity rates rise with inflation. That, in turn, would make biomass electricity more competitive, reducing the required subsidy.

Pressure the Feds

About half of California's forests lie on federal land. Does that mean nothing can be done? Far from it. With Democrats from California presiding over the U.S. Senate and the U.S. House of Representatives, and a sitting president who owes his position to California-based tech billionaires and tech corporations, whatever California really wants from the federal government, California is going to get.

Here's what they should be asking for:

Revise the EPA's "no action" restrictions, usually based on the "single-species management"[121] practice, have led to more than half of California's national forests being off-limits to tree thinning, brush removal, or any other sort of active management.

Change the U.S. Forest Service guidelines which only permit active forest management, even in the areas that are not off-limits, for as little as six weeks per year. While restrictions on when and where forests can be thinned may have sound ecological justifications in some ways, they are making it impossible to thin the forests. The ecological cost/benefits need to be reassessed. To be effective, thinning operations need to be allowed to run for several months each year, instead of several weeks each year.

The EPA needs to streamline the NEPA (National Environmental Policy Act)[122] application process so it is less expensive and time-consuming for qualified companies to get permits to extract timber from federal lands. They can also grant waivers to allow thinning projects to bypass NEPA, or at the least, broaden the allowable exemptions.

The federal government can accelerate granting of long-term stewardship contracts[123] whereby qualified companies acquire a minimum 20-year right to extract wood products from federal lands. This would guarantee a steady supply of wood products which, in turn, would make new investment viable in logging equipment, mills, and biomass energy facilities.

Rules and conditions governing timber exports need revision. The export of raw logs from federal lands in the Western United States is currently prohibited.[124] Lifting this prohibition would help because sawmill capacity is not capable of handling the increase in volume. Just with the new thinning programs already in place, logs and undergrowth are being burned or put in landfills.

As it is, California imports around 80 percent of the cut lumber used in its construction industry or sold through retailers to consumers. If there was an assurance of wood supply—which the national forests can certainly offer—investment would be made in expanding mill capacity. Suddenly the money that is being sent to Oregon, Washington, and British Columbia to purchase their cut timber would stay here in California, employing thousands of workers in the mills.

The state or federal government can set up revolving loan funds[125] for investors to build sawmills, as well as biomass energy facilities, as well as chippers and other equipment, that would allow the industry to quickly ramp up operations and capacity.

Will Politicians Do the Right Thing?

The logic of these steps seems impeccable. Thin the forests. Restore them to ecological health. Adopt time-tested modern logging practices and revive the timber industry. Build biomass power plants on the perimeter of the forests. Reissue grazing permits[126] for additional cost-effective brush thinning. Prevent ridiculous, costly, horrific, tragic wildfires. Help the economy.

But these steps have been known for decades,[127] and nothing has been done. Every time policymakers were close to a consensus on forest thinning, government bureaucrats obstructed the process and the environmentalists sued to stop the process. And they won. Time and time again. And now we have this: millions of acres of scorched earth, air so foul that people couldn't leave their homes for weeks, and wildlife habitat that in some cases may never recover.

California's forest management policies have decimated the state's timber industry, neglected its biomass industry, rejected the cattle industry, turned millions of acres of forest into scorched earth, and are systematically turning mountain communities into ghost towns.

If the goal was to have a healthy forest ecosystem, that was violated, as these forests burned to the ground and what remains is dying. If the goal was to do *anything* in the name of fighting climate change and its impact on the forests and do it with urgency, that too was violated, because everything they did was wrong. Even now, instead of urgent and far-reaching changes to forest management policies, we get more electric car mandates.[128] That was the urgent response to the superfires of 2020.

California's ruling elites, starting with Gavin Newsom among the politicians, and Ramon Cruz,[129] the Sierra Club's new president, may prove they care about the environment by sitting down with representatives from California's timber, biomass energy, and cattle industries, along with federal regulators, and come up with a plan. They might apply to this plan the same scope and urgency with which they so cavalierly transform our entire energy and transportation industries, but perhaps with more immediate practical benefits both to people and ecosystems.

Chapter Eight

Restoring Quality Education

Pragmatism. Abundance. Optimism. If these are the principles that should guide public policy in California—and they are—what the public schools offer is the exact opposite.

Instead of pragmatism, they offer partisan ideology.

Instead of emphasizing the ability, indeed, the *obligation*, for a modern and prosperous society to deliver abundance, the message is that we must ration everything we use, and treat employment as a zero-sum game, where jobs and opportunities are allocated by race and gender instead of in recognition of merit and passion.

And instead of an optimistic view of the future, the mandated curricula are steeped in pessimism: the climate emergency, the crisis of systemic racism, the catastrophe of capitalist enslavement, a sordid national history., and an oppressive, exploitative society.

It isn't necessary to engage in yet another in-depth recitation of how California's public schools have devolved into indoctrination chambers, failing low-income students most in need of a decent education. Rebellion is in the air.

Suffice to say, classroom discipline is replaced with "restorative justice."[130] Teacher accountability, now more than ever, gives way to "tenure" and a job for life. Measuring academic achievement with standardized tests has become racist, and as redress, the University of California will no longer consider applicants' SAT scores.[131] Learning multiplication tables and other practical quantitative skills gave way to "Common Core."[132] Timeless classics may alienate or even threaten young readers, so reading material is selected based on the race and gender of the authors.[133]

Lessons in basic concepts of science are contextualized with the horror of climate change,[134] designed to instill panic. Rather than teaching a generally positive sense of history, students have the "1619 project."[135] And then, starting in the primary grades, there's agenda-driven "gender" curricula.[136]

Two generations of K-12 students have emerged from California's public schools with relatively undeveloped skills in math and English, but steeped in the secular religion of class envy, pointless and bizarre race and gender theory, and a host of related maladies that can be accurately summarized as the politics of resentment, and the rejection of personal responsibility for collective victimhood.

This deception works so well because it creates a monstrous mental distraction, a mind-bending narrative that goes something like this: we are all victims of oppression by the white patriarchy, so naturally we'll assume that our unaffordable homes, lack of good job opportunities, and burning forests are their fault. It won't even occur to us that the people teaching us to hate the white patriarchy are the same people whose policies are truly to blame for the problems we face.

Putting ideology over practical instruction has consequences.[137] In 2019, only half of California's K-12 students met state standards in reading, only 40 percent were proficient in math. The solution, according to California's education experts? Stop testing.[138]

This can change. This *must* change. Discipline does not oppress misbehaving students, it rescues them. Incompetent teachers need to be fired. Tests matter. A command of basic math is an essential life skill and teaching math cannot rely on short cuts or gimmicks. Classics convey universal ideas and passions. The earth is not dying. America is a great nation and we are all lucky to live here. And little children will do just fine if we spare them transgender theory.

Ways to Fundamentally Improve Education in California

Supporters of education reform in California have never had a greater opportunity than right now. More parents than ever have witnessed the selfish overreach of the teachers' unions during the pandemic. They've lost jobs and businesses while the teachers' unions kept schools closed. They've seen, most of them for the first time, what sorts of material teachers were exposing their children to, as remote learning reached into almost every household. And they've experienced, by the millions, creative educational solutions that bypass the traditional public school system.

Change is in the air. Here are some battles that need to be fought.

Implement universal education savings accounts.

The reform that would change everything is universal education savings accounts (ESAs), where the money follows individual students to whatever K-12 school their parents choose for them: traditional public school, charter school, parochial school, private school, or even charter/homeschool and private/homeschool hybrids.

Unchaining the torrent of money that currently pours into traditional public schools without competition and with minimal accountability would be an unprecedented breakthrough. Many of the details of how this could be done have been worked out in SB 1344,[139] introduced by then State Senator John Moorlach in 2018. It would allocate education funds mandated under Proposition 98—the 1988 ballot measure that mandates at least 40 percent of the state's general fund go to K-14 education—into ESAs, assigning an equal amount for every K-12 student in the state. Currently, that is about $14,000 per student per year. Any parent who opted into the program would be able to direct that money to a participating school, whether it's a public, charter, or accredited private or parochial school. Unspent money would accumulate to be used for college, vocational, or any other accredited educational expense.

Empower charter schools.

One of the biggest alternative means of fixing education in California is to empower charter schools. This could be accomplished by broadening the list of entities that can authorize charter schools, permitting charters denied initial opening or renewal applications to appeal to any authorizing entity, removing the cap on how many charter schools can be opened, and prohibiting denial of charter applications or renewals for reasons such as the alleged negative financial impact they may have on traditional public school budgets.

These are big ideas, but there's much more.

Limit union negotiations to pay and benefits and outlaw strikes.

Equally big and disruptive, and beneficial to public education in California, would be to roll back the prerogatives of the teachers' unions. Currently, to quote a well-informed, indignant reformer who prefers anonymity at this time, "these unions can control what color chalk you are allowed to use on the blackboard."

More to the point, the teachers' unions include in their bargaining negotiations things that ought to be up to the district superintendents and the elected school board, such as what textbooks to use. A reform that could go a long way towards fixing public education would be to simply rewrite the education code so unions negotiate over wages and benefits, and nothing more. At the same time, take away their right to strike. Defang the unions.

Change rules governing tenure, layoffs, and dismissal.

Another reform, certain to attract bitter opposition from the teachers' unions, would be simply to change some of the work rules. The *Vergara* case of 2016,[140] which unfortunately failed in the California Supreme Court[141] on a technicality, provides a roadmap. Lengthen a teacher's probationary period before acquiring tenure to at least five years. Replace seniority with merit as the criteria governing which teachers to retain and which to let go in layoffs and downsizings. And greatly streamline the ability to fire incompetent or negligent teachers, so principals can hold them accountable, rewarding good teachers and terminating bad teachers.

Empower parents to opt out of politicized instruction.

A major reform would be to empower parents to remove students from classes that the parents feel violate their beliefs and principles. The new sex education classes, which many parents feel are both inappropriately graphic and tinged with an agenda, are an obvious example, but there are others. Politicized curricula such as the controversial "1619 Project," or critical race theory, are other examples that many parents already oppose. If it were properly formulated, a parent empowerment initiative could be successful. It would allow parents to prevent the indoctrination of their children.

Many national experts in education reform tend to bristle at the idea of wholesale, sweeping changes. But in almost every case, these are activists and lobbyists who worked with legislatures to enact reform. In those situations, the legislature may not have had a sufficient majority of staunch reform advocates to support dramatic changes. Incrementalism was the only possible way forward.

California is a different case. California's legislature will never enact reforms. Pro-charter and pro-school choice advocates in

California's legislature are so outgunned that their mission is merely to reduce the speed at which the teachers' unions accomplish their ever-expanding agenda.

For this reason, the only thing that should matter to education reformers in California is what voters think. California's ballot initiative process is the one final safety valve preventing a complete takeover of the state government by special interests.

A Model School

The reason California needs education reform—school choice, education savings accounts, charter school empowerment, management reforms, work rule reforms, parental rights—is so more schools like the Orange County Classical Academy (OCCA) can open as competitive alternatives.[142]

Despite being one of the most encouraging developments in California's public education in, say, the last 50 years, it is a sad testament to the times we live in that what OCCA does is considered revolutionary. Here is a brief summary of how OCCA differs from every traditional public elementary school in California.

First, they have scrapped the Common Core approach to teaching English and math, and they are making the sex education curriculum "non-pornographic, age-appropriate, and medically accurate." Since Common Core[143] and the recently revised state sex education guidelines[144] have been unpopular with parents and are of dubious value if not actually harmful to students, these are big changes. Moreover, the OCCA's sex education lessons are transparent for parents and the school offers a simple process for parents to opt-out.

Second, OCCA is a licensed operator to use the K-12 curriculum developed by Hillsdale College.[145] Currently, 20 charter schools in 10 U.S. states use the Hillsdale model, which is patterned on the college's own approach to the liberal arts, with a special emphasis on the traditions of Western Civilization. Specifically, the lessons acknowledge America's important role in the world, embracing Judeo-Christian principles as expressed by the American founders. These lessons do not apologize for Western traditions, and will allow all of the students early exposure to the greatest thinkers: Socrates, Plato, Aristotle, Homer, Augustine, and so on.

The students are even taught Latin as their foreign language, with all the benefits and insights early instruction in Latin facilitates: ease in learning any Romance language, and familiarity with the roots of most medical, scientific, and professional terms still in common use.

Third, the way OCCA has coped with the COVID-19 pandemic is based on expert medical advice and unaffected by the opportunistic demands of the teachers' unions.[146] OCCA has been open with no requirement for face coverings for either students or teachers, although all are free to wear them if they wish. The school carried on normal classroom instruction without social distancing or distance learning. The policy is based on virtually all medical data so far showing that COVID-19 is not dangerous to children, and is almost never spread by asymptomatic children, combined with the fact that wearing face masks and enforcing social distancing is harmful to the psyche and the social and intellectual development of children.

None of these revolutionary intentions of OCCA would have happened were it not for a long, bitter fight the organizers had to wage with the teachers' unions and the politicians they control. Charter schools, along with homeschooling, religious schools, and private schools all constitute a mortal threat to the teachers' union monopoly.

What OCCA teaches, promoting Western virtues instead of claiming the West is the scourge of human history and the scapegoat upon which to blame all travails of "disadvantaged" communities, is equally anathema to the teachers' unions.

OCCA's focus on classical education is an audacious, uncompromising challenge to the leftist indoctrination that sadly informs nearly everything taught these days in California's traditional public schools. In an overt slap to the unions, OCCA even intends to include in their instructional materials videos from Prager University,[147] an institution that is loathed by the Left.

Saving Public Education Saves California and Saves America

It's tough to overstate how much fixing K-12 education in California would change *everything*, and it is also tough to overstate just how powerful the teachers' unions will fight against reforms. California's public-sector unions collect and spend nearly $1 billion,[148] mostly in membership dues, *per year*. More than half that money flows into the unions representing teachers and other school employees.

But voter sentiments are changing. California's powerful teachers' unions spent over $20 million last year promoting Proposition 15,[149] which would have increased taxes on commercial properties. Other unions, mostly in the public sector, spent another $17 million to promote Prop. 15. But voters weren't buying it. Prop. 15 failed.

Overall, in November 2020, California's government unions spent nearly $70 million[150] to promote or oppose state ballot measures, and almost all of that spending was unsuccessful. While a couple of union-supported ballot propositions were approved by voters, they weren't high priorities, attracting only around $200,000 in union spending.

This result presents a paradox. Why is it that public-sector unions, which easily wield financial supremacy over any of their political competitors, and use that money to make or break the political campaigns of nearly every member of the California State Legislature, and which in similar manner control nearly every city council, county board of supervisors, school board, and governing board of transit districts and fire districts and transportation districts – why couldn't they impose their will on California's electorate when it came to ballot propositions in 2020?

Consider these results on key initiatives, all contrary to the will of California's government unions: 52 percent of voters rejected increasing property taxes,[151] 56 percent rejected "no bail" laws,[152] 57 percent rejected the reinstatement of racial preferences,[153] 58 percent supported the rights of independent contractors,[154] and 60 percent rejected rent control.[155]

In this paradox there is opportunity. California's voters are no longer the predictable bloc that government unions have relied upon for the past 20 or 30 years. To paraphrase Winston Churchill, the rebellion against union power exemplified by voter rejection of union-supported ballot measures may not be the beginning of the end, but it is definitely the end of the beginning. Voters are finally waking up, fitfully shedding decades of indoctrination.

And why shouldn't they? California has it all—a diverse economy, rich natural resources, deep water ports on the Pacific Rim, the best universities, the epicenter of high tech, and the finest weather on the planet—and yet its governance is a mess. The public schools are failing, the mismanaged forests are burning up, income inequality and poverty are among the worst in America, housing is unaffordable, and the urban downtowns are overrun with drug addicts and predators.

All of this can be quickly fixed by good governance. The answers for correcting these failures are not elusive, nor are they partisan. Repeal extreme environmentalist regulations that have made it impossible to construct affordable housing without subsidies. Restore laws against intoxication, petty theft, and vagrancy, and watch half the homeless population suddenly find shelter with friends and relatives. Help the rest in inexpensive supervised encampments where sobriety is a condition of entrance. Bring back the timber industry to thin the forests and create jobs. But why aren't these fixes implemented?

The reason is equally simple: Government unions, government contractors, powerful "nonprofits," monopolistic corporations, and Big Tech companies acquire power and profit by *never* solving these problems. And along with the insane sums of money they deploy to manipulate public opinion and fund political campaigns, they rely on a thoroughly indoctrinated electorate to support their dysfunction—an electorate that is the product of unionized public schools.

This has been a brilliant scam. But if you change the schools, you change the future. Maybe, just maybe, Californians are ready to demand change.

Chapter Nine

The Prosperity Economy

The policy topics considered in this series—energy, water, transportation, housing, law enforcement and the homeless, forestry, and education—have all been hijacked by ideologues.

Because of this, and regardless of the relevance, climate change and racism are the two broad and urgent themes that dominate policy discussions and decisions on these issues. And in all cases, these alleged crises are used to distort policies and derail projects. They become the primary focus, limiting options, enabling impractical and expensive schemes, and always with a pessimistic outlook. This series has offered a different set of perspectives through which to view these topics: abundance, pragmatism, and optimism.

There are other big challenges that dominate the political dialogue in California and throughout America. It is a broad and diverse list. But the seven topics chosen, if properly addressed, fulfill a practical goal. They give back to Californians—*all* Californians—something that's been missing for decades: a prosperity economy where anyone willing to work hard can afford to live a secure life.

The governing ideology in California today is corporate socialism hiding behind the moral imperatives of fighting climate change and combating racism. California today is run by an alliance of special interests—tech monopolies, public-sector unions, leftist billionaires, extreme environmentalists, and social justice warriors—who are crushing the middle class. Their motivations differ, and their intentions may not be so explicit, but their actions share the same goal. Environmentalists believe the middle-class lifestyle is ecologically unsustainable. Social justice warriors believe the middle class is racist and exclusionary. To the extent small businesses are wiped out and consumers are forced to buy green gadgets and pay more for everything, tech monopolies and billionaires accrue even more wealth and power. Public-sector unions share the ideology of the environmentalists and social justice warriors, and use collective bargaining to largely exempt themselves from the worst consequences afflicting the private sector middle class. But it's all wrong.

Wanting to save the planet and end systemic racism may be legitimate moral concerns. But the policies being implemented in their name are not working. Rationing, redistribution, and retribution are the themes behind current policies. But rationing breeds corruption and squeezes resiliency out of the system. Socialist redistribution destroys incentives, and, not incidentally, socialism managed by mega-corporations is still socialism. It is an authoritarian, centralized system of governing that replaces the competitive, decentralized, and pluralistic economy that is essential to maintaining freedom and prosperity.

Moreover, continuously accentuating the negative aspects of environmental health and race relations is one-sided, punitive, pessimistic, inaccurate, and psychologically unhealthy. We have come so far. We have done so much. Where is that recognition? Where is the optimism?

Practical solutions that lead to abundance need to be the ideology, if you want to call it that, to inform policy on issues affecting prosperity in California—and the United States, for that matter. With abundant desalinated water from the ocean, perpetually recycled wastewater, and storm runoff that's saved for timely release from high dams, environmentalists have more ways to maintain downstream ecosystems and ordinary people can take showers again without worrying about getting fined.

Abundant water and energy provide *resilience* to climate change. Building more suburbs opens up opportunities for *everyone* to achieve homeownership. Enforcing vagrancy laws and laws against hard drugs and petty theft creates a deterrent, pushing individuals towards making healthy choices in their lives. Next-generation roads give *everyone* mobility. Practical education with immutable standards creates uniform incentives, so *everyone* knows that if they can meet the standard they will not be passed over.

The policy recommendations that appeared throughout this series are not written with any attempt to adhere to any conventional ideology. Libertarians and anti-tax activists may object to certain public works projects, particularly with respect to water and transportation. While the recommendations concerning California's energy sector focus primarily on deregulation, and rely mostly on private investment, environmentalists may not accept the argument that California can set a better example to the world by pioneering the cleanest methods possible to use natural gas and nuclear power. Environmentalists will certainly struggle with the solution to forestry management—logging, grazing, and controlled burns—but properly done and privately funded, these enterprises would restore health to the forests and create thousands of jobs.

Public investment is an essential part of any solution to California's punitive cost of living and hostile business environment. By investing in water and transportation infrastructure and deregulating energy production, enabling infrastructure costs less to the end-user. Homebuilders don't have to build into home prices the fees to build the roads and utility conduits. Businesses don't have to pay prices for gas and electricity that are more than double the rates in most other states, and many times the rates in other nations.

There's an important irony to recognize in the calls from both environmentalists and libertarians for the state to *not make* these investments. Why spend $50 billion on civil engineering projects to increase California's annual supply of water to farms and cities by 5 million acre-feet or more? Why not just conserve, and save all that money? Notwithstanding the resiliency argument, which ought to be reason enough, the irony is that the money will still be spent. Instead of wealthier households paying slightly more in taxes, low-income households will have to cover the costs of new "water sipping" appliances that don't work very well, higher water bills, higher electric bills, and more expensive homes to buy or rent. Subsidizing the capital costs for enabling infrastructure yields long-term reductions to the cost-of-living, and distributes those savings to everyone.

There's also an important factor that is too often lost in the panic over climate and race relations, and the rush towards authoritarian solutions to these sudden emergencies: corporate special interests *benefit* when there is scarcity.

Does anyone think the financial firms trading water futures want cheap water? Or that corporate agribusiness doesn't plan to buy every family farm that can't financially withstand consecutive years of drought?

Does anyone think public utilities want to go back to delivering cheap energy, when their profits are pegged by law to a fixed percentage of revenue?

Does anyone think the homeless-industrial complex doesn't love the subsidies attendant to building "permanent supportive housing" on some of the most expensive real estate on the planet? "Inclusive zoning" requires that they locate their projects on land that in some actual cases would sell for over $10 million an acre. This is an outrageous scandal, but if you object, you're a racist. If you're wondering what "corporate socialism" means, this is it.

California's public education curricula, along with California's policies that prevent effective law enforcement, also reflect the corporate socialist mentality. "Restorative justice" is meant to atone for systemic racism and capitalist oppression. Students and criminals alike are victims of society. Better to tell them this lie than admit the reason California is unaffordable is that mega-corporations are rolling up the entire state and turning it into a company town. Don't teach them practical skills, make them angry. Don't punish crimes to create a deterrent to more crime, let them sow chaos. Exploit the unrest to nurture a generation of activists demanding racial justice and environmental justice by any means necessary. Then oblige them. Because no group is easier prey for grifters and demagogues than angry people.

The policies to reverse California's regressive, authoritarian drift require a cultural shift. An awakening. And this awakening requires a movement not of indignation but of *joy*. The only way to convince millions of thoroughly indoctrinated, deliberately embittered and panicked Californians is through *controlled* passion. An unforgettable excerpt from Stephen Vincent Benet's *The Devil and Daniel Webster*[156] provides a cautionary example:

"It was him they'd come for, not only Jabez Stone. He read it in the glitter of their eyes and in the way the stranger hid his mouth with one hand. And if he fought them with their own weapons, he'd fall into their power; he knew that, though he couldn't have told you how. It was his own anger and horror that burned in their eyes; and he'd have to wipe that out or the case was lost."

How do you wipe out anger and horror? How do you erase the negativity that is the currency of the social justice warriors and the climate catastrophists? Facts matter. But to cast light into darkness and change hearts, facts are useless without also presenting a beautiful vision.

The other side can afford hysteria and hate, they can afford to divide their own ranks and eat their own, because it is all smoothed over with rivers of money. Our side can only win if we exude not just tough resolve, but love, compassion, humility, tolerance, and empathy.

This is the power of optimism, the belief that abundance is possible, the suggestion that ideology matters, but sometimes practical solutions matter more. Critics of California's dysfunction accurately describe the problems and the culprits, often with justifiable rage. But there is an irresistible, contagious joy in imagining a future where homes are affordable again, where good jobs are plentiful, where the schools are succeeding and the streets are clean. There is joy in imagining what Californians can do if they have a reliable supply of cheap water and electricity and uncongested roads and freeways. There is joy in imagining the next great leaps in innovation that can come from California—innovation in politics as well as in technology.

Think big. Embrace solutions, but also imagine them realized. Visualize California in just a few decades, heading toward the 22nd century. Imagine a state where abundant energy and water and new, smart roads have enabled megastructures in the urban core and spacious suburbs spreading like penumbra along the interstate corridors. Picture passenger drones and subterranean tunnels crossing the great cities. Spaceplanes carrying passengers from San Francisco to Singapore in 30 minutes.

Consider California, a nation within a state, with mountains and deserts separating it from the rest of America, vast and golden, nestled on the Pacific Rim. Consider California in 2050, with the people fulfilling every bit of their potential and realizing their aspirations, because back in the 2020s and 2030s, Californians had the foresight to invest in massive but practical projects and transformative but sensible policies. This is the prosperity economy. This is the opportunity to advocate today. This is the choice. Anything is possible.

About the Author

Edward Ring is a contributing editor for the California Policy Center, a nonpartisan think tank he co-founded in 2013, and where he served as the first president. He is also a senior fellow with the Center for American Greatness, and a frequent contributor to the California Globe. He is a prolific writer on the topics of political reform and sustainable economic development. His work has appeared in the *Los Angeles Times*, *Wall Street Journal*, *Forbes*, *National Review*, *The Economist*, *Real Clear Politics*, *Politico*, *City Journal*, and other media outlets. He is the author of the book "The Abundance Choice – Our Fight for More Water in California," (2022).

Acknowledgements

Thank you to the Center for American Greatness and the California Policy Center, for their encouragement and for publishing this work in a series of installments during the summer of 2021. Thanks also to the thousands of Californians from all walks of life who demanded, and got, a special gubernatorial recall election and the many candidates for governor of California, all of whom inspired this attempt to focus attention on the issues that truly affect everyone.

Endnotes

Chapter One

[1] *Green Car Reports*, "How will California get to all-electric by 2035," January 22, 2021
https://www.greencarreports.com/news/1131024_how-will-california-get-to-all-electric-by-2035-it-starts-by-breaking-down-barriers
[2] *Inside Climate News*, "California Proposal Embraces All-Electric Buildings," May 8, 2021
https://insideclimatenews.org/news/08052021/california-electric-buildings-natural-gas-ban/
[3] California Energy Commission, "2019 Total System Electric Generation."
https://www.energy.ca.gov/data-reports/energy-almanac/california-electricity-data/2020-total-system-electric-generation/2019
[4] U.S. Energy Information Administration, California State Profile and Energy Estimates.
https://www.eia.gov/state/?sid=CA
[5] Ibid
[6] U.S. Energy Information Administration, Today in Energy
https://www.eia.gov/todayinenergy/detail.php?id=46156
[7] Lawrence Livermore National Laboratory, Estimated California Energy Consumption in 2018
https://flowcharts.llnl.gov/commodities/energy
[8] National Academies of Sciences, Engineering, Medicine: What you Need to Know About Energy: Natural Gas
http://needtoknow.nas.edu/energy/energy-sources/fossil-fuels/natural-gas/
[9] American Automobile Association, How Efficient is Your Car Engine?
https://www.aaa.com/autorepair/articles/how-efficient-is-your-cars-engine
[10] Britannica.com, definition: "quad"
https://www.britannica.com/science/quad
[11] U.S. Energy Information Administration, Units and calculators explained: British thermal units (Btu)
https://www.eia.gov/energyexplained/units-and-calculators/british-thermal-units.php

[12] U.S. Energy Information Administration, State Profile and Energy Estimates: California
https://www.eia.gov/state/data.php?sid=CA
[13] American Physical Society, Physics: Energy Units
https://www.aps.org/policy/reports/popa-reports/energy/units.cfm
[14] University of Calgary, Energy Education, definition: "Watt-hour"
https://energyeducation.ca/encyclopedia/Watt-hour

Chapter Two

[15] Kyle's Converter: Free Conversion Calculators in Your Web Browser
https://www.kylesconverter.com/energy,-work,-and-heat/
[16] California Energy Commission, Electric Generation Capacity and Energy
https://www.energy.ca.gov/data-reports/energy-almanac/california-electricity-data/electric-generation-capacity-and-energy
[17] Statistica, Automobile Registrations in the United States in 2020 by state
https://www.statista.com/statistics/196010/total-number-of-registered-automobiles-in-the-us-by-state/
[18] MojaveDesert.net, The Whole Mojave: Overview
http://mojavedesert.net/description.html
[19] United States Geological Survey, San Joaquin Valley, California
https://pubs.usgs.gov/circ/circ1182/pdf/06SanJoaquinValley.pdf
[20] California Department of Food and Agriculture, "Important Farmland in California, 2002"
https://www.cdfa.ca.gov/agvision/docs/Agricultural_Loss_and_Conservation.pdf
[21] *New Geography*, "America's Most Urban States," March 7, 2016
https://www.newgeography.com/content/005187-america-s-most-urban-states
[22] U.S. Energy Information Administration, Electric Power Monthly, "Average Price of Electricity to Ultimate Customers by End-Use Sector"
https://www.eia.gov/electricity/monthly/epm_table_grapher.php?t=epmt_5_6_a
[23] National Academies of Sciences, Engineering, Medicine: What you Need to Know About Energy: Natural Gas
http://needtoknow.nas.edu/energy/energy-sources/fossil-fuels/natural-gas/

24 *Mongabay*, "Indonesia says no new coal plants from 2023 (after the next 100 or so)," May 12, 2021
https://news.mongabay.com/2021/05/indonesia-says-no-new-coal-plants-from-2023-after-the-next-100-or-so/
25 *Cal Matters*, "Water shortages: Why some Californians are running out in 2021 and others aren't," August 20, 2021
https://calmatters.org/environment/2021/06/california-water-shortage/
26 *American Greatness*, "The Democratic Washing Machine," July 29, 2019
https://amgreatness.com/2019/07/29/the-democratic-washing-machine/
27 California Legislative Information, AB-1434 Urban water use objectives: indoor residential water use, Friedman, February 19, 2021
https://leginfo.legislature.ca.gov/faces/billTextClient.xhtml?bill_id=202120220AB1434
28 Capital Public Radio, "California Water Board Backs Plan To Increase River Flows," December 13, 2018
https://www.capradio.org/articles/2018/12/13/california-water-board-backs-plan-to-increase-river-flows/
29 National Geographic, "Amid Drought, New California Law Will Limit Groundwater Pumping for First Time," September 18, 2014
https://www.nationalgeographic.com/science/article/140917-california-groundwater-law-drought-central-valley-environment-science
30 The Governors' Gallery, Edmund G. Brown Jr., State of the State Address, January 7, 1976
https://governors.library.ca.gov/addresses/s_34-JBrown1.html
31 San Jose Mercury, "California Droughts Have Lasted More Than 200 Years," January 25, 2014
https://www.mercurynews.com/2014/01/25/california-drought-past-dry-periods-have-lasted-more-than-200-years-scientists-say/
32 California Department of Water Resources: State Water Project
https://water.ca.gov/Programs/State-Water-Project
33 Macrotrends: California Population
https://www.macrotrends.net/states/california/population
34 Sites Reservoir Authority: Sites Project
https://sitesproject.org/

35 California Water Commission: Temperance Flat Reservoir Project
https://cwc.ca.gov/Water-Storage/WSIP-Project-Review-Portal/All-Projects/Temperance-Flat-Reservoir-Project
36 Water Education Foundation: San Luis Reservoir
https://www.watereducation.org/aquapedia/san-luis-reservoir
37 U.S. Bureau of Reclamation: Shasta Dam and Reservoir Enlargement Project
https://www.usbr.gov/mp/ncao/shasta-enlargement.html
38 United States Geological Survey: Land Subsidence
https://www.usgs.gov/special-topics/water-science-school/science/land-subsidence
39 California Policy Center, "Rebuilding California's Infrastructure – Desalination," November 23, 2016
https://californiapolicycenter.org/rebuilding-californias-infrastructure-desalination-part-4-of-6/
40 United States Census Bureau, Quick Facts: California
https://www.census.gov/quickfacts/CA
41 California Policy Center, "Towards a Grand Bargain on California Water Policy," August 21, 2018
https://californiapolicycenter.org/towards-a-grand-bargain-on-california-water-policy/
42 California Policy Center, "How to Make California's Southland Water Independent for $30 Billion," August 15, 2018
https://californiapolicycenter.org/how-to-make-californias-southland-water-independent-for-30-billion/

Chapter Four

43 California State Transportation Agency, California Transportation Plan (CTP) 2050
https://dot.ca.gov/-/media/dot-media/programs/transportation-planning/documents/ctp-2050-v3-a11y.pdf
44 Kelly Blue Book, "Lucid Motors Air EV Unveiled," December 15, 2016
https://www.kbb.com/car-news/lucid-motors-air-ev-unveiled/
45 *Business Insider*, "An electric-car battery that can be charged as fast as filling up your gas tank," January 19, 2021
https://www.businessinsider.com/fast-charging-electric-car-battery-5-minutes-2021-1

[46] *Off Grid World*, "Algae Biofuel Farm: Photobioreactor Harvester Extraction System," January 25, 2022
https://offgridworld.com/algae-biofuel-farm-photobioreactor-harvester-extraction-system/
[47] *EE Times*, "Hydrogen Fuel Cell-Powered Drones," January 20, 2021
https://www.eetimes.com/hydrogen-fuel-cell-powered-drones/
[48] California Policy Center, "California's Transportation Future, Part Three – Next Generation Vehicles," May 16, 2018
https://californiapolicycenter.org/californias-transportation-future-part-three-next-generation-vehicles/
[49] California Policy Center, "California's Transportation Future, Part One – The Fatally Flawed Centerpiece," May 8, 2018
https://californiapolicycenter.org/californias-transportation-future-part-one-fatally-flawed-centerpiece/
[50] California Policy Center, "California's Transportation Future, Part Two – The Hyperloop Option," April 18, 2018
https://californiapolicycenter.org/californias-transportation-future-part-two-the-hyperloop-option/
[51] *Travel & Leisure*, "The World's Fastest High-speed Trains," March 23, 2021
https://www.travelandleisure.com/trip-ideas/bus-train/fastest-trains-in-the-world
[52] The Boring Company
https://www.boringcompany.com/tunnels
[53] The Conversation, "How SpaceX lowered costs and reduced barriers to space," March 1, 2019
https://theconversation.com/how-spacex-lowered-costs-and-reduced-barriers-to-space-112586
[54] Kittyhawk
https://www.kittyhawk.aero/history
[55] Aurora Flight Sciences
https://www.aurora.aero/
[56] Vahana
https://acubed.airbus.com/projects/vahana/
[57] Engadget, "Airbus' drone taxi takes to the skies for the first time," February 2, 2018
https://www.engadget.com/2018-02-01-airbus-drone-taxi-first-test-flight.html

[58] Joby Aviation
https://www.jobyaviation.com/
[59] *Investment U,* "Joby Aviation Stock Is Almost Here: What to Know About the SPAC IPO," May 28, 2021
https://investmentu.com/joby-aviation-stock-ipo/
[60] *electrek*, "Audi and Airbus work together on a passenger drone/electric car hybrid," March 6, 2018
https://electrek.co/2018/03/06/audi-airbus-passenger-drone-electric-car/
[61] California Policy Center, "California's Transportation Future, Part Four – The Common Road," July 26, 2018
https://californiapolicycenter.org/californias-transportation-future-part-four-the-common-road/

Chapter Five

[62] Zillow.com, Santa Clara County Home Values
https://www.zillow.com/santa-clara-county-ca/home-values/
[63] CISION PR Newswire "California median home price reaches new all-time high in March as nearly two-thirds of homes sell above asking price, C.A.R. reports," April 16, 2021
https://www.prnewswire.com/news-releases/california-median-home-price-reaches-new-all-time-high-in-march-as-nearly-two-thirds-of-homes-sell-above-asking-price-car-reports-301270683.html
[64] Zillow.com, United States Home Values
https://www.zillow.com/home-values/
[65] Data USA, Santa Clara County, California
https://datausa.io/profile/geo/santa-clara-county-ca/
[66] Public Policy Research Institute, Immigrants in California
https://www.ppic.org/publication/immigrants-in-california/
[67] *Orange County Register*, "First Time Homebuyers are Getting Outbid by Big Companies," April 22, 2021
https://www.ocregister.com/2021/04/22/first-time-homebuyers-are-getting-outbid-by-big-companies/
[68] U.S. Department of Agriculture, Economic Research Service: Major Uses of Land in the United States
https://www.ers.usda.gov/data-products/major-land-uses/major-land-uses/

[69] State Symbols USA: Size of States
https://statesymbolsusa.org/symbol-official-item/national-us/uncategorized/states-size
[70] *New Geography*, "America's Most Urban States," March 7, 2016
https://www.newgeography.com/content/005187-america-s-most-urban-states
[71] *American Greatness*, "The Density Delusion," August 17, 2019
https://amgreatness.com/2019/08/17/the-density-delusion/
[72] Livable California, "SB 9 Fact Sheet: It's Not a Duplex Bill Folks!"
https://www.livablecalifornia.org/sb-9-fact-sheet-2-9-21/
[73] California Policy Center, "The Wondrous, Magnificent Cities of the 21st Century," March 10, 2020
https://californiapolicycenter.org/the-wondrous-magnificent-cities-of-the-21st-century/
[74] *dezeen*, "10 parasitic dwellings that cling to other buildings," September 1, 2017
https://www.dezeen.com/2017/09/01/10-parasitic-architecture-examples-dwellings-roundup/
[75] *Discovery*, "Vertical Farming: Raising Agriculture's Potential and Lowering its Environmental Impact," February 27, 2020
https://www.discovery.com/science/vertical-farming--raising-agriculture-s-potential-and-lowering-i
[76] American Forest Foundation, "Increase Sustainable Wood Supplies."
https://www.forestfoundation.org/what-we-do/increase-sustainable-wood-supplies/

Chapter Six

[77] CBS Los Angeles, "New Federal Report Shows Scope Of California's Homeless Crisis, Over 160K Homeless Prior To Pandemic," March 19, 2021
https://www.cbsnews.com/losangeles/news/california-homeless-population-crisis/
[78] *Associated Press*, "Audit: California should track homeless spending, set policy, February 11, 2021
https://apnews.com/article/california-coronavirus-pandemic-homelessness-dac338003e3f78986bc9369430cddd0b

[79] *Sacramento Bee*, "Which CA cities add new housing, apartment units in 2021?" May 3, 2022
https://www.sacbee.com/news/politics-government/capitol-alert/article260983777.html
[80] *Cal Matters*, "California's population shrank in 2020, but don't call it an exodus," May 7, 2021
https://calmatters.org/politics/2021/05/california-population-shrink-exodus/
[81] *American Greatness*, "America's Homeless Industrial Complex," July 13, 2019
https://amgreatness.com/2019/07/13/americas-homeless-industrial-complex/
[82] California Policy Center, "The Boondoggle Archipelago," November 20, 2019
https://californiapolicycenter.org/the-boondoggle-archipelago/
[83] *FindLaw, "Jones v. City of Los Angeles"*
https://caselaw.findlaw.com/us-9th-circuit/1490887.html
[84] Ballotpedia: California Proposition 47, Reduced Penalties for Some Crimes Initiative (2014)
https://ballotpedia.org/California_Proposition_47,_Reduced_Penalties _for_Some_Crimes_Initiative_(2014)
[85] Ballotpedia: California Proposition 57, Parole for Non-Violent Criminals and Juvenile Court Trial Requirements (2016)
https://ballotpedia.org/California_Proposition_57,_Parole_for_Non-Violent_Criminals_and_Juvenile_Court_Trial_Requirements_(2016)
[86] California Legislative Information: AB-109 Criminal justice alignment.(2011-2012)
https://leginfo.legislature.ca.gov/faces/billNavClient.xhtml?bill_id=20 1120120AB109
[87] *Cal Matters*, "Why is it so hard to get mentally ill Californians into treatment? Three bills tell the tale," August 29, 2018
https://calmatters.org/health/2018/08/california-homeless-mental-illness-conservatorship-law/
[88] California Legislative Information: The Lanterman-Petris-Short Act
https://leginfo.legislature.ca.gov/faces/codes_displayexpandedbranch .xhtml?tocCode=WIC&division=5.&title=&part=1.&chapter=&article=
[89] KQED, "Should S.F. Be Able to Compel Mentally Ill Homeless People Into Treatment?" April 25, 2019
https://www.kqed.org/news/11742865/should-s-f-be-able-to-compel-mentally-ill-homeless-people-into-treatment

90 California Legislative Information: SB-1045 Conservatorship: serious mental illness and substance use disorders.(2017-2018) *https://leginfo.legislature.ca.gov/faces/billTextClient.xhtml?bill_id=20 1720180SB1045*

91 KQED, "Should S.F. Be Able to Compel Mentally Ill Homeless People Into Treatment?" April 25, 2019 *https://www.kqed.org/news/11742865/should-s-f-be-able-to-compel-mentally-ill-homeless-people-into-treatment*

92 *Los Angeles Times*, "Could a San Francisco experiment be an answer to L.A.'s sprawling street encampments?" May 7, 2021 *https://www.latimes.com/homeless-housing/story/2021-05-07/san-francisco-tests-campsites-homelessness-solution*

93 *City Journal*, "Seattle Under Siege," Autumn 2018 *https://www.city-journal.org/seattle-homelessness*

94 Ballotpedia, George Gascon *https://ballotpedia.org/George_Gascon*

95 Ballotpedia, Chesa Boudin *https://ballotpedia.org/Chesa_Boudin*

96 *City Journal*, "Broken Windows Works," May 29, 2019 *https://www.city-journal.org/broken-windows-policing-works*

97 Solutions for Change, "Solving family homelessness- One family, one community at a time." *https://solutionsforchange.org/*

98 *San Diego Union-Tribune*, "Solutions for Change ends drug testing, programs at some housing projects," October 25, 2020 *https://www.sandiegouniontribune.com/news/homelessness/story/20 20-10-25/solutions-for-change-severs-from-county-program*

99 HUD Exchange: Homeless Emergency Assistance and Rapid Transition to Housing Act *https://www.hudexchange.info/homelessness-assistance/hearth-act/*

100 California Legislative Information: AB-953 Law enforcement: racial profiling.(2015-2016) *https://leginfo.legislature.ca.gov/faces/billNavClient.xhtml?bill_id=20 1520160AB953*

101 National Alliance to End Homelessness, "Racial Inequalities in Homelessness, by the Numbers," June 1, 2020 *https://endhomelessness.org/resource/racial-inequalities-homelessness-numbers/*

102 *City Journal*, "Broken Windows Works," May 29, 2019
https://www.city-journal.org/broken-windows-policing-works
103 LexisNexis, Law School Case Brief, "Jones v. City of Los Angeles - 444 F.3d 1118 (9th Cir. 2006)"
https://www.lexisnexis.com/community/casebrief/p/casebrief-jones-v-city-of-l-a-444-f-3d-1118-9th-cir-2006
104 MoralFoundations.org: Moral Foundations Theory
https://moralfoundations.org/

Chapter Seven

105 Berkeley Public Library, "The Story of the Berkeley Fire," January 21, 1924
https://www.berkeleypubliclibrary.org/sites/default/files/files/inline/bplhstrm_979.467_st76_the_story_of_the_berkeley_fire.pdf
106 DisaasterPhilanthropy.org: 2020 North American Wildfire Season
https://disasterphilanthropy.org/disasters/2020-california-wildfires/
107 States and Symbols USA: Size of U.S. States
https://statesymbolsusa.org/symbol-official-item/national-us/uncategorized/states-size
108 ABC 30 Action News, "Creek Fire: 379,895 acres burned," November 22, 2020
https://abc30.com/creek-fire-shaver-lake-firer/8174281/
109 *Fresno Bee*, "Decades of controlled burns save Shaver Lake from Creek Fire, "September 24, 2020
https://www.fresnobee.com/opinion/opn-columns-blogs/marek-warszawski/article245842780.html
110 @GavinNewsom: "You don't believe in climate change. You are excused from this conversation," November 3, 2019
https://twitter.com/GavinNewsom/status/1191032777463889920?emci=8521489e-faff-e911-828b-2818784d6d68&emdi=a889227c-fcff-e911-828b-2818784d6d68&ceid=7883562
111 *Politico*, "JERRY BROWN to Congress: 'Get with it, or get out of the way'," October 30, 2019
https://www.politico.com/newsletters/california-playbook/2019/10/30/trump-operative-papadopolous-files-for-ca25-katie-hill-seat-jerry-brown-to-congress-get-with-it-or-get-out-of-the-way-ncaa-follows-cas-lead-on-student-athletes-gig-companies-unveil-ballot-play-more-power-outages-extreme-santa-ana-winds-487547

[112] Congressman Tom McClintock, "Our Forests Tragedy," September 23, 2020
https://mcclintock.house.gov/newsroom/speeches/our-forests-tragedy
[113] *California Globe*, "California is On Fire Again and it was Preventable," September 8, 2020
https://californiaglobe.com/articles/california-is-on-fire-again-and-it-was-preventable/
[114] Congressman Tom McClintock, "About the District"
https://mcclintock.house.gov/about/our-district
[115] U.S. Census Bureau: 113th Congress of the United States, California Congressional District 4
https://www2.census.gov/geo/maps/cong_dist/cd113/cd_based/ST06/CD113_CA04.pdf
[116] United States Department of Agriculture, California's Forest Products Industry and Timber Harvest, 2012
https://www.fs.fed.us/pnw/pubs/pnw_gtr908.pdf
[117] *California Globe*, "California is On Fire Again and it was Preventable," September 8, 2020
https://californiaglobe.com/articles/california-is-on-fire-again-and-it-was-preventable/
[118] *Fresno Bee*, "Decades of controlled burns save Shaver Lake from Creek Fire, "September 24, 2020
https://www.fresnobee.com/opinion/opn-columns-blogs/marek-warszawski/article245842780.html
[119] *Science*, "To save forests, cut some trees down, scientists say," April 21, 2017
https://www.science.org/content/article/save-forests-cut-some-trees-down-scientists-say
[120] Science Daily, "Billions of gallons of water saved by thinning forests," April 24, 2018
https://www.sciencedaily.com/releases/2018/04/180424160251.htm
[121] Yale School of the Environment, "Conservation Conundrum: Is Focusing on a Single Species a Good Strategy?" May 17, 2018
https://e360.yale.edu/features/conservation-conundrum-is-focusing-on-a-single-umbrella-species-a-good-strategy
[122] U.S. Environmental Protection Agency: Summary of the National Environmental Policy Act, 42 U.S.C. §4321 et seq. (1969)
https://www.epa.gov/laws-regulations/summary-national-environmental-policy-act

[123] U.S. Forest Service: Stewardship Contracting Overview
https://www.fs.fed.us/restoration/Stewardship_Contracting/overview.shtml
[124] U.S. Forest Service: Log Export Restrictions of the Western States and British Columbia
https://www.fs.fed.us/pnw/pubs/pnw_gtr208.pdf
[125] Council of Development Finance Agencies: Revolving Loan Funds & Development Finance
https://www.cdfa.net/cdfa/cdfaweb.nsf/pages/revolving-loan-funds.html
[126] Public Lands Council, "Interrupting the Catastrophic Fire Cycle," March 21, 2021
http://publiclandscouncil.org/wp-content/uploads/2021/03/Wildfire.pdf
[127] *Napa Valley Register*, "Senator Feinstein Blames Sierra Club for Blocking Wildfire Bill," November 2, 2002
https://napavalleyregister.com/news/sen-feinstein-blames-sierra-club-for-blocking-wildfire-bill/article_5f3818fe-a67a-593c-8835-03d6d3ce724e.html
[128] Office of Governor Gavin Newsom, "Governor Newsom Announces California Will Phase Out Gasoline-Powered Cars & Drastically Reduce Demand for Fossil Fuel in California's Fight Against Climate Change," September 23, 2020
https://www.gov.ca.gov/2020/09/23/governor-newsom-announces-california-will-phase-out-gasoline-powered-cars-drastically-reduce-demand-for-fossil-fuel-in-californias-fight-against-climate-change/
[129] Sierra Club: "Ramón Cruz Elected First Latino President of the Sierra Club," May 19, 2020
https://www.sierraclub.org/articles/2020/05/ram-n-cruz-elected-first-latino-president-sierra-club

Chapter Eight

[130] *Investors Business Daily*, "Undisciplining Kids Through 'Restorative Justice'," January 9, 2014
https://www.investors.com/politics/editorials/education-department-advises-schools-to-adopt-restorative-justice/

131 University of California, San Diego, *The Guardian*, "UC Agrees to No Longer Consider ACT/SAT Scores in Admissions," May 23, 2021 *https://ucsdguardian.org/2021/05/23/uc-agrees-to-no-longer-consider-act-sat-scores-in-admissions/*

132 Pinterest.com, For Every Mom, "This Dad Just Taught His Kids' School an Unforgettable Lesson About Common Core Math." *https://www.pinterest.com/pin/476185360583823778/*

133 The New Press: 12 Books for Anti-Racist K-12 Education, June 11, 2020 *https://thenewpress.com/blog/reading-lists/12-books-for-anti-racist-k-12-education*

134 *American Educator*, "Teaching Climate Change," Winter 2019-2020 *https://www.aft.org/sites/default/files/ae-winter2019-2020.pdf*

135 Pulitzer Center, The 1619 Project Curriculum. *https://pulitzercenter.org/lesson-plan-grouping/1619-project-curriculum*

136 Public Health Post, "The Genderbread Person 3.0." *https://www.publichealthpost.org/databyte/genderbread-person/*

137 *Cal Matters*, "California kids' test scores again rise by inches as achievement gap yawns," October 9, 2019 *https://calmatters.org/education/k-12-education/2019/10/california-schools-test-scores-2019-achievement-gap-caaspp-smarter-balanced/*

138 *EdSource*, "Hundreds of thousands of California students won't take statewide standardized tests this spring," May 4, 2021 *https://edsource.org/2021/hundreds-of-thousands-of-california-students-wont-take-statewide-standardized-tests-this-spring/654123*

139 California Legislative Information: SB-1344 Education expenses: Education Savings Account Act of 2020.(2017-2018) *https://leginfo.legislature.ca.gov/faces/billTextClient.xhtml?bill_id=20 1720180SB1344*

140 California Policy Center, "Vergara v. the State of California," August 23, 2016 *https://californiapolicycenter.org/tag/vergara-vs-the-state-of-california/*

141 *EdSource*, "California high court lets rulings stand on teacher tenure, school funding lawsuits," August 22, 2016 *https://edsource.org/2016/state-supreme-court-declines-to-hear-vergara-inadequate-funding-cases/568350*

142 Orange County Classical Academy
https://orangecountyclassicalacademy.org/
143 *San Jose Mercury News*, "Common Core: Did Parents Get Left Behind?" June 17, 2018
https://www.mercurynews.com/2018/06/17/common-core-did-parents-get-left-behind/
144 *The Daily Signal,* "California Implements Extreme New Sex Ed Curriculum," July 9, 2019
https://www.dailysignal.com/2019/07/09/california-implements-extreme-new-sex-ed-curriculum/
145 Hillsdale Academy: Educational Philosophy
https://academy.hillsdale.edu/Academic-Program/
146 California Policy Center, "The Looming School Reopening Nightmare," June 2, 2020
https://californiapolicycenter.org/the-looming-school-reopening-nightmare/
147 Prager University
https://www.prageru.com/
148 California Policy Center, "California's Public Sector Unions Rake in $921 Million in Annual Revenue," August 5, 2020
https://californiapolicycenter.org/californias-public-sector-unions-rake-in-921-billion-in-annual-revenue/
149 Ballotpedia: California Proposition 15, Tax on Commercial and Industrial Properties for Education and Local Government Funding Initiative (2020)
https://ballotpedia.org/California_Proposition_15,_Tax_on_Commercial_and_Industrial_Properties_for_Education_and_Local_Government_Funding_Initiative_(2020)
150 California Policy Center, "Government Unions and California Ballot Propositions," December 17, 2020
https://californiapolicycenter.org/government-unions-and-california-ballot-propositions/
151 Ballotpedia: California Proposition 15, Tax on Commercial and Industrial Properties for Education and Local Government Funding Initiative (2020)
https://ballotpedia.org/California_Proposition_15,_Tax_on_Commercial_and_Industrial_Properties_for_Education_and_Local_Government_Funding_Initiative_(2020)

[152] Ballotpedia: California Proposition 25, Replace Cash Bail with Risk Assessments Referendum (2020)
https://ballotpedia.org/California_Proposition_25,_Replace_Cash_Bail _with_Risk_Assessments_Referendum_(2020)
[153] Ballotpedia: California Proposition 16, Repeal Proposition 209 Affirmative Action Amendment (2020)
https://ballotpedia.org/California_Proposition_16,_Repeal_Propositio n_209_Affirmative_Action_Amendment_(2020)
[154] Ballotpedia: California Proposition 22, App-Based Drivers as Contractors and Labor Policies Initiative (2020)
https://ballotpedia.org/California_Proposition_22,_App-Based_Drivers_as_Contractors_and_Labor_Policies_Initiative_(2020)
[155] Ballotpedia: California Proposition 21, Local Rent Control Initiative (2020)
https://ballotpedia.org/California_Proposition_21,_Local_Rent_Contro l_Initiative_(2020)

Chapter Nine

[156] Goodreads.com: *The Devil and Daniel Webster*, by Stephen Vincent Benét, first published January 1937
https://www.goodreads.com/book/show/992073.The_Devil_and_Dani el_Webster